The Essence of Linguistic Analysis

Linguistics

Volumes published in this Brill Research Perspectives title are listed at *brill.com/rplis*

The Essence of Linguistic Analysis

An Integrated Approach

By

R. M. W. Dixon

BRILL

LEIDEN | BOSTON

Library of Congress Control Number: 2021901251

Typeface for the Latin, Greek, and Cyrillic scripts: "Brill". See and download: brill.com/brill-typeface.

ISSN 2667-0682
ISBN 978-90-04-44650-2 (paperback)
ISBN 978-90-04-44651-9 (e-book)

Copyright 2021 by R. M. W. Dixon. Published by Koninklijke Brill NV, Leiden, The Netherlands.
Koninklijke Brill NV incorporates the imprints Brill, Brill Hes & De Graaf, Brill Nijhoff, Brill Rodopi, Brill Sense, Hotei Publishing, mentis Verlag, Verlag Ferdinand Schöningh and Wilhelm Fink Verlag. Koninklijke Brill NV reserves the right to protect this publication against unauthorized use. Requests for re-use and/or translations must be addressed to Koninklijke Brill NV via brill.com or copyright.com.

This book is printed on acid-free paper and produced in a sustainable manner.

Contents

Preface   VII
Acknowledgements   IX
Abbreviations   X
Abstract   1
Keywords   1
Introduction   1
1   Preliminaries   2
2   The Basic Scheme   3
   2a   *Types of Clause*   3
   2b   *Phrases Filling Slots in Clause Structure*   4
   2c   *Transitivity Classes of Verbs*   6
   2d   *Distinguishing A and O Arguments*   7
   2e   *Marking Core Arguments*   9
   2f   *'Accusative' and 'Ergative' Labels*   13
   2g   *Phrase Structure*   14
   2h   *Word Formation*   15
   2i   *The Storeys and Their Different Characters*   17
3   Semantic Types and Semantic Roles   18
4   Peripheral Arguments   25
   4a   *Marking of Peripheral Arguments*   25
   4b   *Meaning of Peripheral Arguments*   30
   4c   *Extended Intransitive and Extended Transitive Clause Types*   32
5   Clauses within Phrases and Clauses within Clauses   35
   5a   *Relative Clauses*   36
   5b   *Complement Clauses*   37
   5c   *Complement Clauses and Semantic Roles*   41
   5d   *Conclusion*   44
6   Free and Bound Pronouns   45
   6a   *The Heterogeneous Class of Pronouns*   45
   6b   *Pronouns and Nouns*   48
   6c   *Bound Pronouns*   49
   6d   *The Limited Role of Bound Pronouns*   53
7   Head of a Verb Phrase   55
   7a   *Varieties of Structure for a Verb Phrase*   55
   7b   *Something Other Than a Verb as Head of a Verb Phrase*   59

8 Copula Clauses and Verbless Clauses 60
    8a *Contrasting Copula Complement with Non-verbal VP Head* 64
9 Types of Intransitive Subject, S 65
    9a *Split-S Marking* 66
    9b *Fluid-S Marking* 67
10 The Sentence and Above 71
    10a *The Syntax of Clause Linking* 71
    10b *The Semantics of Clause Linking* 73
    10c *Above the Sentence* 75
    Commentary and Notes 77
    Preliminary Note 78
    Notes to Sections 79
    References 81
    Index 83
    Books by R. M. W. Dixon 86

Preface

Many works on linguistic typology deal in some detail with one or more particular grammatical topics without clearly demonstrating how these relate to other categories or construction types.

The purpose of the present volume is to present a framework which connects individual topics in a cogent and coherent way, showing their dependencies and locating each in its place within the overall tapestry of a language.

Over the years there have been a range of sound typological expositions commencing with the classic works titled *Language* by Sapir (1921) and Bloomfield (1933), extending to the two editions of *Language Typology and Syntactic Description* (Shopen 1985, 2007) and *The Cambridge Handbook of Linguistic Typology* (Aikhenvald and Dixon (2017), plus many works by other authors. Especially relevant are my three-volume work *Basic Linguistic Theory* (BLT) and Alexandra Aikhenvald's *The Art of Grammar, a Practical Guide* (AoG).

It must be emphasized that *The Essence of Linguistic Analysis: An Integrated Approach* is in no way a competitor to nor a replacement for these volumes. Rather it should be seen as complementary to them. Each of the topics included in *Essence* is dealt with in considerable detail in, for example, BLT and/or AoG, but it was only indirectly shown there how they are linked together. Those links are exposed and explained in *Essence*.

There are two overriding principles which underlie the exposition here.

First, stress is placed on the distinction between:
(a) Semantics, with roles such as 'agent' and 'patient' (see section 3); and
(b) Syntax, with functions such as 'transitive subject', 'intransitive subject', and 'transitive object', and case marking conventions such as 'nominative' and 'accusative' or 'absolutive' and 'ergative'. It is important not to confuse these; for instance, misleadingly talking of 'agent case', or 'patient case', or things similar.

Secondly, the fundamental dictum which is followed is that the basic constituents of a language are lexical elements. Grammatical items serve to link together lexical units. At every level of analysis, the central units are lexical with grammar providing ancillary indicators.

Essence is not conceived of as an introductory text. Rather it is a consolidation, for students of linguistics who already have a fair knowledge of the subject. The intended audience is those who have studied BLT, or AoG, or similar works by other authors

In no sense is *Essence* a condensation of the 1,300-plus pages of BLT. Each chapter of BLT provides a comprehensive account of a particular grammatical topic (for example, negation, possession, transitivity), with statement of the parameters involved, illustrated from a wide range of languages. If the reader wishes to get a full characterisation of, say, copula clauses and verbless clauses, they should consult chapter 14 of BLT, volume 2. Section 8 of *Essence* summarises some major points in order to relate these construction types to other techniques of saying a similar thing; for instance, using an intransitive construction with a non-verbal predicate.

Essence differs from BLT in one significant way. BLT aimed to provide a conspectus of each grammatical topic within a cross-linguistic perspective, with illustrations from a wide range of languages. In contrast, *Essence* simply seeks to delineate the crucial nature of each topic considered. Where possible, example sentences are taken from English, or else from other languages which I know well (having done extensive fieldwork on them). Otherwise, exemplification is provided from appropriate languages. In only a few places are examples repeated from BLT.

It was not considered appropriate in BLT and AoG to include too much mention of recent unwarranted innovations, such as regarding the preposition as head of a peripheral noun phrase. Throughout *Essence* there are comments which contrast the standard approaches in linguistic analysis, which are espoused here, with other attitudes. References have not been provided as to which scholar put forward which proposal (often several—sometimes many—people did so). The aim has not been to engage in debate, but rather to provide clarification.

What is described in *Essence* is, basically, the way in which most grammars of minority languages have been analysed over the past decades. *Essence* attempts to set forth a consistent general exposition of widely-accepted ideas, which have been tested by time.

Acknowledgements

Alexandra Aikhenvald inspired this essay and provided invaluable feedback. I am also most grateful for the detailed comments provided by Nerida Jarkey, Luca Ciucci, Katarzyna Wotjylak, and René van den Berg; and for the more general ones from Anne Storch, Hannah Sarvasy, Lars Johanson, and Peter Matthews. Brigitta Flick and Joelene Overall provided valuable assistance in proof-checking.

Abbreviations

1	1st person
2	2nd person
3	3rd person
A	transitive subject function
ABS	absolutive case
ACC	accusative case
ANATEG	*A New Approach to English Grammar, on Semantic Principles* (Dixon 1991)
AoG	*The Art of Grammar: A Practical Guide* (Aikhenvald 2005)
ASATEG	*A Semantic Approach to English Grammar* (Dixon 2015)
ART	article
BLT	*Basic Linguistic Theory*, vols. 1–3 (Dixon 2010–2012)
CA	common argument in a relative clause construction
CAUS	causative
CC	copula complement function
CoCl	complement clause
COMIT	comitative
CS	copula subject function
DAT	dative case
DEC	declarative
du	dual
E	extension to core
ERG	ergative case
f	feminine
INST	instrumental
IPr	intransitive predicate
LOC	locative
m	masculine
Mf	marker attached to focal clause
Ms	marker attached to supporting clause
NOM	nominative case
nonfem	non-feminine
NP	noun phrase
O	transitive object function
pl	plural
RC	relative clause
REP	reported
S	intransitive subject function

ABBREVIATIONS

Sa	S marked in the same way as A
sg	singular
So	S marked in the same way as O
TPr	transitive predicate
VCC	verbless clause complement function
VCS	verbless clause subject function
VP	verb phrase

The Essence of Linguistic Analysis
An Integrated Approach

R. M. W. Dixon
  Language and Culture Research Centre, James Cook University,
  Cairns, Queensland, Australia
  robert.dixon@jcu.edu.au

Abstract

Many works on linguistic typology deal in some detail with one or more particular grammatical topics without clearly demonstrating how these relate to other categories or construction types. *The Essence of Linguistic Analysis* presents a framework which connects individual topics in a cogent and coherent way, showing their dependencies and locating each in its place within the overall tapestry of a language. Alongside the recurrent cross-linguistic framework, attention is paid to non-canonical associations such as nominals functioning as predicates, and split- and fluid-S marking. A clear distinction is made between semantic roles and syntactic functions. And it is held that the basic constituents of a language are lexical elements. Grammatical items serve to link together lexical units. At every level of analysis, the central units are lexical with grammar providing ancillary indicators. There is a commentary on ersatz theoretical approaches which obscure the underlying template of a language.

Keywords

grammar – syntax – semantics – syntactic arguments – semantic roles – transitivity – relative clauses – complement clauses – copula clauses – free and bound pronouns – split-S – fluid-S

Introduction

My aim here is to provide a clear, consistent and integrated approach to linguistic analysis. This is simply an outline. References are provided, in the Commentary and Notes, to works which give detailed expansion for many of the topics mentioned here.

A   There are a variety of current ideas about linguistic analysis, often inconsistent one with another, and frequently lacking in perspective. Quite often a principle is suggested which on the surface seems cute and nifty but on examination involves over-generalisations, and glosses over significant structural differences within and between languages. Comments on these are included throughout, each identified by a letter, and by a vertical line on the right-hand side of the comment.

1   Preliminaries

Note that this is the merest outline, indicating basic make-up. There are three components to a language:
- *Lexical words* (or *lexemes*), which have reference. Most refer to observable things, activities, states, and properties, some to abstract states. They can be divided into word classes (a.k.a. 'parts of speech'). Word classes are recognised on the basis of internal grammatical criteria within that language. The major word classes are open; that is, new members can be added to them, by internal derivation within a language, or by taking over words from another language ('borrowing' of 'loan' words).
- *Grammar*, which has three parts:
    - Constructions: with slots into which fit lexical constructs. (A lexical construct can be a single lexeme, or a specified combination of lexemes.) For example an intransitive main clause involves an intransitive subject slot, filled by a noun phrase, and an intransitive predicate slot, filled by an intransitive verb phrase.
    - Grammatical elements, or ordering conventions, which mark the functions of lexical constructs. For example: a case system, adpositions, ordering of constituents within a clause.
    - Grammatical systems (always closed, with a limited number of members, which cannot be extended) that add elements of meaning. For example, definiteness, gender, tense.

    Lexemes are the crucial ingredients of a language. Grammar is secondary to them. Each constituent is centred on a lexeme or lexemes.
- *Phonology* is the method a language evolves for communicating intertwined lexical and grammatical information from speaker to hearer. A limited number of abstract units of sound ('phonemes') are recognised, such that if one of these is substituted for another there is a change in meaning. The ways in which these are pronounced is phonetics. Put simply, phonology describes

the channel of communication, phonetics the physical mechanism of speaking.

Alongside spoken languages there are also sign languages which operate with gestures and postures of the hands, head, face, lips, etc., instead of units of sound.

We here focus just on lexicon and grammar.

2 The Basic Scheme

The full picture will be built up gradually. In this section we begin with the skeleton, as it were, and in later sections gradually add more, finally producing a well-rounded scheme of analysis.

2a *Types of Clause*

The central element in language is the clause. Clauses can be combined into larger units: sentence and discourse; these are discussed in section 10.

The primary constituent of a clause is the predicate. The choice of predicate comes first and determines what else is included.

Each clause has a number of core constituents, which are needed to complete the clause. There may, optionally, be a number of peripheral constituents, which serve to expand its meaning; these are discussed in section 4.

Each language has two major clause types:
- *Intransitive clause*, whose core components are an intransitive predicate (abbreviated to 'IPr') and one core nominal argument (traditionally called 'intransitive subject', conveniently abbreviated as 'S').
- *Transitive clause*, whose core components are a transitive predicate (abbreviated to 'TPr') and two core nominal arguments (traditionally called 'transitive subject', conveniently abbreviated as 'A', and 'transitive object', conveniently abbreviated as 'O').

Thus at the level of *clause*, there are two main *structures*:
- intransitive predicate plus S argument
- transitive predicate plus A argument and O argument

B Some linguists take '*sentence*' as the basic unit. In fact it is '*clause*'. A sentence may have several linked clauses each of which could be used on its own; there may also be a number of subordinate clauses. A 'main clause' by itself may constitute a (minimal) sentence.

C   Some linguists follow the practice of mediaeval philosophers in regarding each sentence as having two parts: *subject*, the argument in S or A function, and *predicate*, which covers everything else (including the O argument in a transitive clause, and all peripheral arguments, adverbs, etc.). The more usual practice is that followed here—to distinguish between core (obligatory) and peripheral (optional) constituents, and to treat an argument in O function on a par with those in S and A functions.

In some languages, there is a measure of association between TPr and O; for instance, in English an adverb may not intervene between TPr and O. However, overall the three core arguments (A, S and O) are best regarded as direct constituents of a clause. Some grammatical operations link together S and A, others S and O (and both linkages may be found in a single language).

D   Since in most European languages, arguments in S (intransitive subject) and A (transitive subject) functions have similar properties, they have often been treated as identical and labelled just as 'S'. Cross-linguistically, S and A are far from identical. And even in English, a highly 'accusative' language, it is important to distinguish the three core arguments. For example, derivational suffix *-less* forms an adjective relating to S for an intransitive verb (*rest-less*, *relent-less*), to A for some transitive verbs (*harm-less*, *resist-less*) and to O for other transitive verbs (*count-less*, *use-less*).

E   A habit has arisen of characterising a language, in terms of the order of constituents, as SOV or SVO, etc. Or—recognising a distinction between A and S—as AOV, SV or AVO, SV, or AVO, VS, etc. This is muddling labels: A, S and O describe functions of core arguments within a clause, while V is a word class. The label corresponding to A, S and O would be 'predicate'. An appropriate characterisation would be along the lines of: A-TPr-O, IPr-S, and so on.

2b   Phrases Filling Slots in Clause Structure

The slots in clause structure are filled by types of phrases:
- *Intransitive predicate* (IPr) slot will prototypically be filled by an intransitive verb phrase (VP) which has as its head an intransitive verb.
- *Transitive predicate* (TPr) slot will be filled by a transitive verb phrase (VP) which has as its head a transitive verb.
- *Argument slots* will prototypically be filled by noun phrases (NPs) which each has as its head a noun.

Thus, whether the verb that is head of the VP predicate slot is intransitive or transitive determines whether the clause requires one core argument (in S function) or two core arguments (in A and O functions).

In many languages core argument slots are always filled by NPs and the intransitive predicate slot is always filled by a VP. However, some languages do allow for other possibilities. The regular correspondences in Mandarin Chinese are shown in (1) and (2) (where *le* is a sentence-final particle 'currently relevant state'):

(1) [Daifu]   [lai]   le
    doctor   come   PARTICLE
    S:NP   IPr:VP
    The doctor came

There is a variant on this pattern, where a VP can function as S argument:

(2) [Lai]   [dui]   le
    come   be.right   PARTICLE
    S:VP   IPr:VP
    Coming was right (that is: It was right to come)

Nootka, a Wakashan language spoken on Victoria Island in British Columbia, allows the same variation on the standard pattern, and also permits an NP to function as intransitive predicate. The regular correspondences are shown in:

(3) [ʔi·ḥ-ma·]   [qo·ʔas-ʔi·]
    be.large-3sg.INDICATIVE man-ARTICLE
    IPr:VP   S:NP
    The man is large

For the variant pattern in (4), the NP is marked as an IPr and the VP is marked as an S argument:

(4) [qo·ʔas-ma·]   [ʔi·ḥ-ʔi·]
    man-3sg.INDICATIVE   be.large-ARTICLE
    IPr:NP   S:VP
    The large one is a man

For Mandarin Chinese, Nootka, and other languages which show variations of this type, the great majority of clauses employ the regular correspondences

S : NP and IPr : VP, as in (1) and (3). But the variants do occur in a minority of instances, and cannot be ignored.

F One common (but simplistic) approach to analysis works with formulas such as:

> Sentence (by which is meant Clause) → NP (meaning NP in S or A function) + VP (meaning Intransitive Predicate, or Transitive Predicate plus NP in O function)

Firstly, this continues the old habit of dividing a clause into subject and predicate (everything else) but without using these labels, and restricting VP (predicate) just to everything else in the core (but not including peripheral arguments). This approach assumes that an S or A argument slot is always filled by an NP; it typically is but not always.

It is vital to distinguish between an element of clause structure and its phrasal filler. At the least, the formula should go, for prototypical instances:

> Intransitive clause → S : NP + IPr : VP
> Transitive clause → A : NP + TPr : VP + O : NP

This would allow for variations, such as S : VP and IPr : NP, to be treated in a straightforward way.

2C *Transitivity Classes of Verbs*

In some languages every (or almost every) verb has strict transitivity; Latin and the Australian language Dyirbal are of this type. That is, a verb is either intransitive, occurring just in an intransitive clause, or transitive, occurring just in a transitive clause.

In other languages many verbs are ambitransitive, and can be used in both intransitive and transitive clause structures: English is like this.

The varieties of transitivity can be illustrated for English:
- Some verbs are strictly intransitive and may only be used in an intransitive clause. For example, *go* in:

(5) [The soldier]$_{\text{NP:S}}$ [has gone]$_{\text{VP:IPr}}$

Noun *soldier* is head of the NP in S function and verb *go* is head of the VP in IPr function.

– Some verbs are strictly transitive and may only be used in a transitive clause. For example, *take* in:

(6) [The soldier]$_{NP:A}$ [has taken]$_{VP:TPr}$ [the red car]$_{NP:O}$

Noun *soldier* is head of the NP in A function, noun *car* is head of the NP on O function and verb *take* is head of the VP in TPr function.
– Many verbs are ambitransitive, and may be used in both intransitive and transitive clauses. For example:

(7) [The soldier]$_{NP:S}$ [has eaten]$_{VP:IPr}$
(8) [The soldier]$_{NP:A}$ [has eaten]$_{VP:TPr}$ [his lunch]$_{NP:O}$

For *eat*, the S argument for the intransitive clause relates to the A argument for the transitive one. This class of verbs are 'S = A ambitransitive'. Now consider something a little different:

(9) [The ice]$_{NP:S}$ [has melted]$_{VP:IPr}$
(10) [The hot sun]$_{NP:A}$ [has melted]$_{VP:TPr}$ [the ice]$_{NP:O}$

For *melt*, the S argument for the intransitive clause relates to the O argument for the transitive one. This class of verbs are 'S = O ambitransitive'.

Note that whether an ambitransitive verb is of type S = A or of type S = O depends on the meaning of the verb.

G Some linguists try to explain away the existence of ambitransitive verbs along the following lines (having very much in mind the grammar of English). An S = A ambitransitive verb is basically transitive but may sometimes omit its O argument (they don't say under what conditions). An S = O ambitransitive verb is also basically transitive, and when used intransitively is in a quasi-passive construction (although it is quite different from an actual passive). This is awkward at best; in most circumstances it is absolutely unworkable.

2d Distinguishing A and O Arguments

The core components of an intransitive clause are an intransitive predicate (IPr), which is prototypically realised by a VP, and an argument in intransitive subject (S) function, realised by an NP. If we are told that the phrasal components are *ran away* and *the fat boy* we know, from the meanings of the phrases, that the first is in S and the second in IPr function, making up a clause *The fat boy ran away*.

The core components of a transitive clause are a transitive predicate (TPr), which is prototypically realised by a VP, and two arguments, each realised by an NP. Suppose that the phrasal components are *embraced*, which by its meaning must be TPr, plus *the fat boy* and *an old lady*. What we need to know is who did what to whom? Did an old lady embrace the fat boy, or were things the other way round?

Every language has a technique for resolving this question through identifying one core argument of a transitive clause as being in A function and the other as being in O function. The criteria for recognising these are:
– *Transitive subject (A) is the core argument whose referent*—generally a person or animal, sometimes a natural phenomenon or thing—*has the potential to initiate or control the activity or state involved.*
– *Transitive object (O) is the other core argument in a transitive clause.* The referent of the O argument may be physically or mentally affected by the activity, but not always so.

It is a notable feature of human languages, from across the world, that they show consistency in the way the two core arguments of a transitive clause are distinguished.

The referent of an NP in S function for an intransitive clause may sometimes initiate or control the activity or state, other times not so. This depends on the nature of the VP functioning as IPr, and the context of use. For example subjects for *go, jump, stand*, and *work* will normally be exercising control, but not those for *fall, laugh, shudder*, and *die*. However, this is not a cut-and-dried matter—for example, laughing is typically involuntary, but it may on occasion be purposeful.

H   Some approaches to linguistic analysis fail to distinguish between syntactic functions and semantic roles. They employ the label 'A', but say that it stands for 'Agent' (a semantic role) rather than Transitive Subject (a syntactic function). Also that 'O' indicates 'Patient'; indeed, 'P' may be used in place of 'O'. This semantic restatement does not hold water. Consider:

   [The girl]$_A$ saw$_{TPr}$ [a flash of lightning]$_O$

It could scarcely be maintained that *the girl* is here an Agent, nor that *a flash of lightning* is a Patient.

The desirability of clearly distinguishing between syntactic functions and semantic roles is the topic of section 3.

2e Marking Core Arguments

There must be some means for marking which core argument of a transitive clause is in A and which is in O function. One function could have overt marking with the other being left unmarked. Or both could receive a non-zero marking. We also need to consider the S argument of an intransitive clause. It may be marked in the same way as A, or in the same way as O, of differently from both.

Languages are in many ways parsimonious. No language is presently known which has three separate markings—for A, O and S—across its whole grammar. Generally, S is either marked in the same manner as A, or else in the same manner as O. There are established names for the schemes of marking associated with these alternatives, as shown in the diagram:

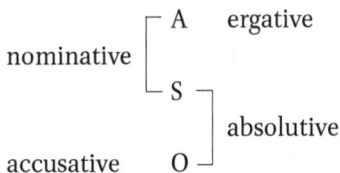

We saw in the last section that in some instances S is like A (its referent initiating or controlling the activity or state) and in some instances like O (not doing so). It is thus natural that in some languages S should be marked in the same way as A, and in others in the same way as O.

(A more satisfactory arrangement would be for S to be marked like A when this is appropriate, and like O in other circumstances. Some languages do, in fact, have such 'split-S' or 'fluid-S' marking; they are discussed in section 9.)

There are three main techniques for marking core arguments.

(a) By the order of phrasal constituents in the clause. English employs this technique for its nominative/accusative scheme—an NP in A or S function precedes the predicate, and one in O function follows it. (In addition most pronouns have two forms—nominative *I, he, she, we, they,* and accusative *me, him, her, us, them.*)

(b) Rather than relying on the ordering of phrases, syntactic function may be marked by small grammatical elements or adpositions; these may be prepositions, preceding the NP, or postpositions, following it. Japanese is like English in operating with a nominative/accusative scheme, but uses postpositions: nominative *ga* for S and A functions and accusative *o* for O function, as in:

(11) [Jone ga]$_A$ [Mary o]$_O$ but-ta$_{TPr}$
John NOMINATIVE Mary ACCUSATIVE hit-PAST
John hit Mary

(12) [Mary ga]$_A$ sin-da$_{IPr}$
Mary NOMINATIVE die-PAST
Mary died

(c) In some languages there is a system of case inflections, used to mark core and also peripheral nominal arguments. Each NP must select one term from the system. The inflectional affix may go on every word in the NP, or just the last word, or just the head word. The Dravidian language Malayalam follows a nominative/accusative scheme for its case inflections. Nominative case is unmarked (or, one could say that it has zero realisation) and accusative case is shown by accusative inflection -(y)e. For example:

(13) kurtti$_A$ amma-ye$_O$ yirliccu$_{TPr}$
child mother-ACCUSATIVE call.PAST
The child called the mother

(14) amma$_S$ vannu$_{IPr}$
mother come.PAST
The mother came

(In fact accusative suffix -(y)e is only used if the referent of the O argument is animate; otherwise the O argument is left unmarked, just like A and S arguments.)

The Australian language Dyirbal also has a case system for nouns and this utilises the absolutive/ergative scheme. Absolutive (for S and O functions) is unmarked while ergative (for A function) is shown by case suffix -ŋgu.

(15) [guda midi]$_O$ [yara-ŋgu jami-ŋgu]$_A$ [balga-n]$_{TPr}$
dog:ABS small:ABS man-ERG fat-ERG hit-PAST
The fat man hit the small dog

(16) [guda midi]$_S$ juda-ñu$_{IPr}$
dog:ABS small:ABS run.away-PAST
The small dog ran away

A case suffix marks the function of an NP in a clause; in Dyirbal it goes onto every word of the NP.

Both absolutive and ergative can have non-zero marking, as can both nominative and accusative in the other scheme. If one case has zero realisation in the absolutive/ergative set-up it is always absolutive. If one case has zero realisation in the nominative/accusative set-up it is almost always nominative. This is, in each instance, the case which includes S function is unmarked.

(However, there are just a few exceptions for the nominative/accusative scheme, with nominative—which covers S and A—receiving non-zero marking—and accusative—for O—remaining unmarked.)

I   A persistent error is to refer to order of phrasal constituents within a clause as 'word order' (as if every phrase consisted of just one word), rather than 'constituent order'. Often, when a language is said to have 'free word order', what is meant is that phrasal constituents may occur in any order within a clause. Some languages do have actual free word order, meaning that words may occur in any order within a clause.

The distinction between 'free (phrasal) constituent order' and 'free word order' is crucial and often not properly appreciated. It can be exemplified from Dyirbal. We can look back at sentence (15). Free constituent order would mean that the phrases, enclosed within square brackets, may occur in any order without affecting the meanings of the sentence. For example: *yara-ŋgu jami-ŋgu guda midi balga-n*. Dyirbal has this and it also has free word order, which means that the five words may appear in any order, with words from different phrases being interspersed. For example: *jami-ŋgu guda yara-ŋgu balga-n midi*. From the case endings (or lack of endings) on nouns and adjectives one can tell which belong together in a noun phrase. Whichever of the 120 possible orderings of words is chosen, the meaning always is 'The fat man hit the small dog'.

In some languages, case marking, which shows syntactic function—is morphologically integrated with some other category, of a quite different nature. In Latin, for example, both nominative and accusative have non-zero marking and they are fused with the category of number; that is, whether the NP has singular or plural reference. Thus, for a masculine noun from the second declension, the case/number inflectional suffixes are:

	singular	plural
nominative (S and A)	-us	-ī
accusative (O)	-um	-ōs

Example sentences, with nouns *domin-* 'master' and *serv-* 'slave' are:

(17) domin-us$_S$ ven-it$_{IPr}$
 master-NOMINATIVE:SINGULAR comes
 The master comes

(18) serv-ī$_A$ domin-um$_O$
 slave-NOMINATIVE:PLURAL master-ACCUSATIVE:SINGULAR
 aud-iunt$_{TPr}$
 hear
 The slaves hear the master

The purpose of a language is to express and communicate meaning. The aim of linguistic analysis is to uncover and describe the underlying structures and systems, as they organise the basic semantics of what is said or written. This underlying matrix is then mapped onto what is called 'surface structure'. Not infrequently, two entirely different bits of information may be blended together in surface structure, as here in Latin when one nominal suffix fuses *number*, which relates to the *referent* of the NP and *case*, which specifies the *syntactic function* of the NP in the clause.

Inflectional affixes to a verb in Latin can be even more all-embracing. Suffix *-it* on *ven-* 'come' in (17) combines the following bits of information: 3rd person singular subject (in S or A function), present tense, active voice, and indicative mood. Suffix *-iunt* on *aud-* 'hear' in (18) differs just in that it indicates plural number rather than singular number of 3rd person subject. These elements of meaning come from six quite different underlying systems—*number* and *person* (reference) of *subject* (syntactic function), *tense* (another kind of reference), *voice* (type of syntactic construction), and *mood* (variety of speech act).

There is *no underlying connection* between the six specifications; they just happen to be expressed together through a single suffix in the surface structure of Latin, a highly fusional language. Their amalgamation in surface structure carries no semantic significance. The same applies to the fusion of information about case and number in nominal suffixes.

Some linguists attempt just to analyse surface structure. They achieve only a limited understanding of the nature of a language, of its intrinsic properties and potentialities, of its underlying meanings and their interconnections. Meaning is what it is all about.

2f 'Accusative' and 'Ergative' Labels

In order to maintain clarity and avoid confusion, one should always take care to avoid using one label for what are several rather different phenomena.

'Accusative(/nominative)' and 'ergative(/absolutive)' describe the two common schemes for marking core arguments of a clause. These labels are also appropriate for characterising certain conditions on the linking together of clauses. For some languages, if two clauses share an argument which is in S or A function in each, it may be omitted from the second clause. English is like this. Consider (where '∅' represents zero, an omitted constituent):

(19) [The fat man]$_A$ hit [the small dog]$_O$ and ∅$_S$ ran away

The unstated S NP of the second clause is inferred to be the same as the A NP of the first clause since English works with an S/A pivot for clause linking; that is, it was the fat man who ran away.

In contrast, Dyirbal operates with an S/O pivot. Clauses (15) and (16) may be combined with the S NP omitted from the second clause since it is the same as the O NP of the first clause. Here it is the small dog who ran away.

(20) [guda   midi]$_O$ [yara-ŋgu   jami-ŋgu]$_A$ [balga-n]$_{TPr}$ ∅$_S$
      dog:ABS   small.ABS   man-ERG   fat-ERG   hit-PAST
      juda-ñu$_{IPr}$
      run.away-PAST
      The fat man hit the small dog and the small dog ran away

Since these conditions on clause-linking relate directly to syntactic functions, and are language-specific, it is appropriate to call an S/O pivot 'ergative syntax' and an S/A pivot 'accusative syntax'.

There are a number of other ways in which S and A may function in a similar manner, irrespective of whether a language has an accusative or an ergative case-marking and/or clause-linking profile. They include:
- A canonical imperative may omit a 2nd person subject, whether in S or A function.
- When a concept such as 'can', 'try' or 'begin' is shown by a verb which is linked to a referential verb, they must have the same subject, whether S or A.

Although S and A are associated here, and in quite a few other ways, these are quite different from morphological and syntactic accusativity, so that it is inappropriate (and confusing) to label them as 'accusative'.

There are also a number of other ways in which S and O may function in a similar manner, irrespective of whether a language has an accusative or an ergative case-marking and/or clause liking profile. They include:
- Many languages have ambitransitive verbs of type S = O, as illustrated in (9–10).
- Some word derivations relate just to S and O arguments. An example from English involves suffix *-ee*. Applied to a transitive verb, it derives a noun which describes the referent of the O argument for the verb; for example, *employ-ee* and *invit-ee*. With an intransitive verb the derived noun relates to the S argument; thus *escap-ee* and *retir-ee*.

Although S and O are associated here, and in a fair number of other ways, these are quite different from morphological and syntactic ergativity, so that it is inappropriate (and confusing) to label them as 'ergative'.

2g Phrase Structure

A phrase corresponds to a slot in clause structure. Generally, a noun phrase (NP) relates to an argument slot (S or A or O) and a verb phrase (VP) to the predicate slot. This is always the prototypical situation. However, as mentioned in section 2b, some languages also have secondary correspondences—NP in intransitive predicate slot and/or VP in argument slot. Section 7b discusses non-verbs functioning as head of a VP.

Each phrase has a lexeme as its head. It may, optionally be modified by other lexemes. Consider the sentence (using 'M' as an abbreviation for 'Modifier'):

(21) [Clever$_M$ young$_M$ student-s$_{HEAD}$]$_{NP}$ [just$_M$ study$_{HEAD}$]$_{VP}$
      [difficult$_M$ problem-s$_{HEAD}$]$_{NP}$

The head lexeme is the core of each phrase. It can be used alone, without modification, as in:

(22) Student-s study problem-s

Properties of the phrase, as a whole, are determined by the head. The two NPs in (21) are plural because the head noun is plural. In other languages, with grammatical gender, the gender of an NP is the gender of its head; this may be reflected in gender agreement on the predicate. The VP in (21), *just study*, is transitive because its head verb is here used in its transitive sense (*study* is in fact an S = A ambitransitive verb).

A noun as NP head is typically modified by adjectives, such as *clever, young, difficult*. In addition, some nouns may be used as modifiers, as in *metal*$_M$ *box*$_{HEAD}$ or *boy*$_M$ *king*$_{HEAD}$. A verb as VP head is typically modified by adverbs, such as *just, probably, almost, quietly*. It may also be modified by an auxiliary verb such as *can* (as in *Students* [*can*$_M$ *study*$_{HEAD}$]$_{VP}$ *problems*).

A phrase may require some grammatical specification. For example, in English number must be specified for a head noun of the 'countable' subclass—either singular, which is unmarked, or plural, shown orthographically by *-s*. Also an, NP with a countable head must be marked as definite—by article *the*—or indefinite—shown by *a(n)* when singular, and with zero marking when plural or generic, as in (21–22).

A VP in English requires obligatory grammatical specification for tense. This goes on the first word of the auxiliary modifier, if there is one—present *can study* versus past *could study*—otherwise on the head verb itself—present *studies* (3sg subject) or *study* (other subject) versus past *studied*.

This is a just a preliminary outline of the structure of phrases. There may be a phrase within a phrase; for example a possessive phrase in [[*the old lady's*]$_{NP}$ *little dog*]$_{NP}$. The head of an NP may be a pronoun or a demonstrative; languages vary concerning whether a pronoun or demonstrative head may take modifiers.

The aim has been to show that every phrase has a lexeme as its head, and it is this which determines the properties of the phrase as a whole.

2h   Word Formation

Lexical words (lexemes) correspond to the slots in phrase structure—head and modifier. In some languages no changes are made to the lexical root. In others, processes of derivation and inflection may apply. A word is then built up as follows:

– Commence with a lexical root.
– Optionally apply a derivational process to the root. This may involve adding an affix, or internal modification (an English example is noun *song* from verb *sing*), or shifting stress, or changing tone, etc. The derivational process may sometimes retain word class (adjective *tame-able* from adjective *tame*) and sometimes change it (noun *moist-ure* from adjective *moist*). A derivational process applied to a root produces a stem. (A root with no derivational additions is a minimal stem.)

  Any number of derivational processes may be applied. Each produces a new stem.

– After all derivational processes have been applied, the final stem must receive an obligatory inflection appropriate to its word class. For example, if an English word just consisted of the countable noun root *person* it must take number inflection—this is an obligatory choice from the number system—becoming either singular, *person*, or plural, *person-s*. The derived stem *person-ify*, which is a verb, must take verbal inflection—present *person-ify/person-ifie-s*, past *person-ifi-ed*, etc.

This can be illustrated by following through the formation of *de-myth-olog-ise-er-s*:

(23)
noun root	myth	'traditional tale, often partly imaginative'
derived noun stem	myth-ology	'collection of myths'
derived verb stem	myth-olog-ise	'interpret something as a myth'
derived verb stem	de-myth-olog-ise	'distinguish fact from myth'
derived noun stem	de-mytholog-is-er	'someone who distinguishes fact from myth'
inflected word	de-myth-olog-is-er-s	'several of such people'

Myth and *mythology* are nouns and will take plural inflection, like *demythologiser*. *Mythologise* and *demythologise* are verbs and will require a choice from the system of verbal inflection (tense etc.).

Components of word structure are called 'morphemes'. *De-myth-olog-is-er-s* consists of six morphemes—a noun root, one derivational prefix, three derivational suffixes, and one inflectional suffix.

In this example the components are readily segmentable (as shown by hyphens). However, this is not always possible. For instance, the past tense inflection of verb *take* is *took*, and the plural inflection of noun *man* is *men*, both involving internal change. And in some languages one affixal element may combine several bits of information; this was illustrated in section 2e for Latin. For example, in (17) *-it* is a portmanteau verbal suffix combining six morphemes—3rd person, plus singular number, plus subject (S or A) function, plus present tense, plus active voice, plus indicative mood.

A lexical root can be either 'free', able to occur on its own, or 'bound', always requiring an inflectional affix (or for some other type of inflectional process to have applied). Adjectives are free roots in English. Noun and verb roots could be said to be free, but only because one choice (singular) in the obligatory system of number inflection on nouns is formally unmarked, as is one choice (present tense, for non-3sg subject) in the obligatory system of verbal inflection. In Latin all lexical roots are bound, requiring a non-zero inflection.

2i The Storeys and Their Different Characters

A language can be viewed as akin to an edifice consisting of several storeys, each having a distinct character. A middle storey is 'clause', with those below being 'phrase' and 'word'. What has been said above about these can now usefully be diagrammed (including just the prototypical clause-structure-slot-to-phrase correspondences). Upper storeys—sentence and discourse—are brought into the discussion in section 10.

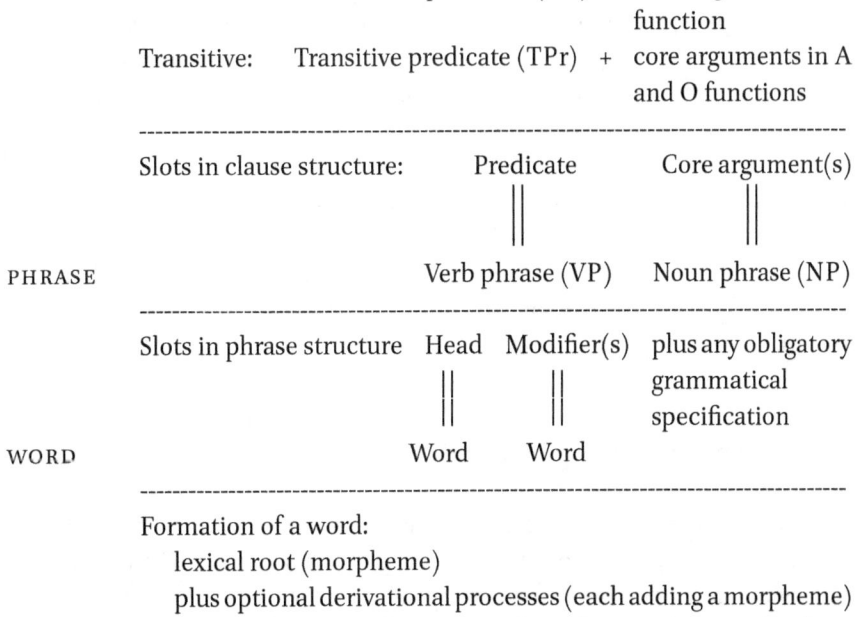

Formation of a word:
  lexical root (morpheme)
  plus optional derivational processes (each adding a morpheme)
  plus an obligatory choice from the inflectional system for that word class, if the language has this (a final morpheme)

The storeys differ in several ways:
- For a *clause*, all the core components are necessary—predicate and core argument(s). (Note that these will either be explicitly stated, or else understood from the textual and situational context.)
- For a *phrase*, only the lexical head is necessary (plus any grammatical specification required by the language, as an accessory).

- A free root may constitute a full *word*. But in many languages, grammatical specification appropriate to the word class of the root (a bound root) is needed.

Note also that each clause and each phrase easily divides into its components. But, as we have seen, a word may be segmentable into its constituent morphemes—as shown by hyphens in (23), for example—or may not be.

There is a central element in each storey, but these are significantly different.
- The *predicate* is the primary constituent of a clause. It is the transitivity of the predicate which determines the number of core arguments. And the clause requires these; it cannot consist of just a predicate with no mention of its arguments.
- The *head* is the only obligatory constituent of a phrase and provides the grammatical profile (number, gender, etc.) for the whole phrase.
- The *root* is the foundation of a word, on the basis of which the whole structure is created. The word class of the root determines what derivations may be applied.

J   In an attempt to devise a homogeneous analysis, it has been suggested that the predicate has the same role for a clause as the head does for a phrase and the root for a word, over-extending the term 'head' to cover all of them. Such a simplistic approach misses a great deal of the structural intricacy of a language.

3   Semantic Types and Semantic Roles

Section 2 was concerned basically with grammar. It is now time to relate this to the semantic foundations of a language. The important point to bear in mind is that syntactic functions and semantic roles are conceptually distinct. We need to study the ways in which one relates to the other, but care must be taken not to implicitly merge them.

In section 2a we saw how the choice of predicate determines the character of a clause. If the predicate slot is filled by a VP with a transitive verb as its head, then the clause will have two core arguments, in A and O functions. If the VP has as its head an intransitive verb—or, as we shall see in section 7, an NP or adjective or pronoun as head—then the clause will have one core argument, in S function. We will now show how the semantic type of the verb determines the semantic nature of the NPs which relate to core argument slots.

3 SEMANTIC TYPES AND SEMANTIC ROLES

Every language covers a wide range of meanings. The great majority of these are similar between languages, being augmented by culture-specific ideas appropriate to each particular society.

Verbs describe a variety of kinds of activities and states. These can usefully be grouped into a number of *'semantic types'*, such that verbs in each type have a common meaning component and similar grammatical possibilities. We can illustrate with some of the recurring semantic types from English; other languages follow similar patterns.

For each semantic type, the verbs require a number of *'semantic roles'*. For instance, verbs from the GIVING type need specification of three semantic roles—Donor, Gift, and Recipient—in order to complete a statement of an instance of the activity.

We can usefully illustrate a selection of seven recurrent semantic types involving transitive verbs and the semantic roles associated with them:

Semantic type	Semantic roles			
(i) AFFECT (for example, *hit, burn*)	Agent	Target		
(ii) GIVING (for example, *give, lend*)	Donor	Gift	Recipient	
(iii) THINKING (for example, *remember*)	Cogitator	Thought		
(iv) DECIDING (for example, *choose, select*)	Decision-maker	Course		
(v) ATTENTION (for example, *see, hear*)	Perceiver	Impression		
(vi) SPEAKING (for example, *speak, tell*)	Speaker	Message	Addressee	Medium
(vii) LIKING (for example, *like, love, hate*)	Experiencer	Stimulus		

Each transitive clause has a core argument in A (transitive subject) function and another in O (transitive object) function. In English, and in almost every language, it is the semantic role in the left-hand column of the roles section of the table (set off from the other roles by a dotted line) which relates to syntactic function A. Why should it be that—although they refer to different kinds of participants in the respective activities—Agent, Donor, Cogitator, Decision-maker, Perceiver, Speaker, and Experiences should all correspond to syntactic function A?

An explanation for this was suggested in section 2d:
– *Transitive subject (A) is the core argument whose referent*—generally a person or animal, sometimes a natural phenomenon or thing—*has the potential to initiate or control the activity or state involved.*
– *Transitive object (O) is the other core argument in a transitive clause.* The referent of the O argument may be physically or mentally affected by the activity, but not always so.

To justify the explanation, the seven semantic types illustrated in the table can be briefly discussed, one by one.

(i) **The AFFECT type**. Plainly the Agent role (in A function) is in control. For example, *She hit her brother, He swept the floor, The soldiers dug a trench.* The Agent will normally be human but could be a natural phenomenon; in *The typhoon knocked the house down* it is the typhoon which initiates the activity. The Agent could also be some object. as in *The falling branch hit me*. The Target role (in O function) is in most cases physically affected—her brother is hurt, the floor is cleaned, the trench has been created, the house is no more, and I am injured.

(ii) **The GIVING type**. The act of giving is necessarily initiated and controlled by the Donor, which thus relates to A function. What is of particular interest here is that there are two other essential roles—Gift and Recipient. Either could be in O function. Indeed, in English there are two constructions, one for each alternative:

(1) [The doctor]$_{DONOR:A}$ gave [some pills]$_{GIFT:O}$ [to John]$_{RECIPIENT}$
(2) [The doctor]$_{DONOR:A}$ gave [John]$_{RECIPIENT:O}$ [some pills]$_{GIFT}$

In (1) the Gift is in O function and the Recipient takes preposition *to*, which generally marks a peripheral argument but is used for what is essentially a third core argument of this semantic type. (This is discussed in section 4.) The construction in (2) is rather unusual (for English) in having two post-predicate NPs each with no marking—the O argument (here Recipient role) is followed by the Gift role, also with no marking.

The roles in O function could only be said to be 'affected' by the activity in a rather indirect manner—the gift is transferred from one ownership to another, and the recipient gains possession of the gift. Basically,

3 SEMANTIC TYPES AND SEMANTIC ROLES

a role which does not initiate or control the activity is in O function, and here there are two candidates.

For some languages only the Gift can be in O function and for others only the Recipient. Others have two verbs, one for each alternative.

(iii) **The THINKING type.** It is clearly the Cogitator who both initiates and controls the activity, and so is placed in A syntactic function. The Thought, as the other role, is placed in O function but it is not in any way affected by the activity. Example sentences are: *Grace imagined a great disaster*, *Michael knows the names of all the presidents*, and *George has always believed the Pope*.

(iv) **The DECIDING type.** The Decision-maker role must relate to syntactic function A, since it is responsible for the activity. In a sentence such as *The boss appointed Lucy as Production Controller*, it is plain that Lucy—the other role, the Course, mapped onto syntactic function O—is affected by the appointment. In *Clarence selected a Saab as his new car*, one could just about say that the Saab was affected (it would now be owned by Clarence). But in *Mary chose Wednesday as the day for the meeting*, there is no way in which Wednesday is affected by this choice.

(v) **The ATTENTION type.** For *look at* and *listen to* (which each functions like a transitive verb) it is plain that the Perceiver concentrates their attention to initiate and control the activity. The same applies for other verbs from this semantic type, including *observe, notice, recognise, discover,* and *watch*. But what of *see* and *hear*? One cannot help hearing a noise, nor help seeing something which appears in the field of vision; there is no control involved here. The Perceiver for *hear* and *see* is linked to syntactic function A because (i) these verbs are unfocussed relatives of *listen to* and *look at*. Also (ii) there can be—although there need not be—some control involved. If advance notice is given of something passing by, or of a noise booming out, then one can shut one's eyes or cover one's ears to avoid seeing or hearing it. (Negative control, but control all the same.)

The Impression is placed in O function simply because it is the other semantic role. It is seldom likely to be affected by the activity. Not in *He listened to the concert*, or *She witnessed the accident*, or *We heard the explosion*. In *They discovered a seam of gold* then the seam of gold is not now affected but may soon be (when miners arrive to dig it out).

(vi) **The SPEAKING type.** There can here be four semantic roles, although it is only the Speaker role which is obligatory. Indeed, one can have an intransitive clause [*The President*]_SPEAKER:S *spoke next.*

With Speaker in A function, any of the other roles may be in O function, depending on the choice of verb. For example:

(3) Message as O   The President spoke the truth   The actor told a joke
(4) Addressee as O The President told her husband   The actor informed his agent
(5) Medium as O   The President spoke French   The actor mispronounced French

All four roles can be combined in one clause:

(6) [The President]_SPEAKER:A explained [the situation]_MESSAGE:O [to her husband]_ADDRESSEE [in French]_MEDIUM

It is plainly the Speaker who initiates/controls the activity and is in A function. The non-Speaker role which is focussed on in this instance of use is placed in O function with the other roles being marked by appropriate prepositions. (A role may be in O slot to satisfy syntactic linkage at sentence or discourse level.) We can enquire whether the referent of any of the non-Speaker roles might be affected by the activity. The Message or Medium could scarcely be, but the Addressee might well be mentally affected, as in *The manager scolded/praised the clerk.*

(vii) **The LIKING type.** Whereas the six semantic types just discussed are found—in varying but recognisable form—in just about every language, the verb type LIKING, as in English, has a more limited distribution. (These ideas are expressed by adjectives in some languages.)

Verbs from this semantic type have two roles, Experiencer and Stimulus. While the Stimulus is entirely passive, it is possible that the referent of the Experiencer—who will be a person or maybe a higher animal—may control (perhaps in an indirect way) the state referred to by the verb. If one hears *Samantha likes opera*, then plainly Samantha can place herself in a position to satisfy this liking (she goes to the opera, or listens to recordings). The Experiencer will thus be in A function with the other role, the Stimulus, being in O function.

3 SEMANTIC TYPES AND SEMANTIC ROLES

But it does not have to be this way. English has another semantic type of verbs (which can be called the ANNOYING type) where things are reversed—Stimulus is A and Experiencer is O. We can compare the two types with some sample members:

Semantic type	Experiencer role	Stimulus role	Sample verbs
LIKING	A function	O function	like, love, hate prefer, loathe, worship
ANNOYING	O function	A function	please, entertain, annoy, anger, worry

For ANNOYING verbs the Experiencer simply submits to the state; it is the referent of the Stimulus role which has the potentiality for controlling what happens. In *Ted's shouting annoys the neighbours*, the neighbours do not control or initiate the state to which they are subjected. Ted may or may not be shouting on purpose to annoy them; in any case he could control his shouting. Plainly, for this and other verbs from the ANNOYING type, the Stimulus must be placed in A function; then the other role, the Experiencer, goes into O function.

Consider sentences with verbs which have comparable meanings: *like* from the LIKING type and *please* from the ANNOYING type:

(7) Ernest$_{\text{EXPERIENCER:A}}$ liked [Mary's dancing]$_{\text{STIMULUS:O}}$
(8) [Mary's dancing]$_{\text{STIMULUS:A}}$ pleased Ernest$_{\text{EXPERIENCER:O}}$

For (7), Ernest experienced a feeling of pleasure. Mary may or may not have been aware that Ernest was watching her dance. If she had been aware and put on her best show to provide Ernest with maximum pleasure, then it would be appropriate to say (8). Mary—in the Stimulus role—was now controlling the activity, and the Stimulus role is thus linked to syntactic function A. The Experiencer, as the non-controlling (or 'other') role, is in O function.

The referents of semantic roles. We saw before that the transitivity of the verb which is head of the VP in predicate slot determines how many arguments the clause has. It has now been shown how the semantic type to which this verb belongs will determine what may be heads of the NPs in core syntactic functions within the clause.

Very roughly, the possibilities include, for English:
- Human being (or perhaps anthropomorphised machine): Cogitator, Speaker
- Human or higher animal: Perceiver, Experiencer
- Human or higher animal or natural phenomenon or thing: Agent
- Human or human organisation: Donor, Decision-maker
- Human or higher animal or human organisation: Addressee

This is meant simply to be suggestive of the possibilities involved.

Summary. Syntax and semantics are distinct levels of analysis which must be kept apart. An example of their relationship can be diagrammed:

SYNTAX	Transitive predicate (TPr)	A argument	O argument
	↑	↑	↑
==========	↑	↑	↑
	↑	↑	↑
SEMANTICS	Verb from the ATTENTION semantic type	Perceiver semantic role	Impression semantic role

There will be diagrams along these lines for every semantic type. (English has the eight illustrated above and a dozen more.)

We have given, as the criterion for recognising a semantic role to be relating to A (transitive subject) function at the level of syntax: 'that role whose referent has the potential to initiate or control the activity or state involved'.

Is there any other way of characterising the semantic roles which are linked to A? 'Agent', in its usual sense, is someone or something which 'produces an effect'. Agent role for the AFFECT type clearly produces a physical effect. One could, with some difficulty, make a case that there may be an agentive element for Donor, Decision-maker, and Speaker. But not, surely, for Cogitator, Perceiver, or Experiencer.

The role (or one of the roles) that is not linked to A function will be in O function at the syntactic level. The referent of this role can, for some semantic types, be physically or mentally affected by the activity. This may be so for the Target in the AFFECT type and perhaps for the Gift and the Recipient in the GIVING type, sometimes for the Course in the DECIDING type and for the Addressee in the SPEAKING type. But the referents of other roles would not be affected; this applies for Thought, Impression, Message, Medium, and Stimulus.

K As mentioned in comment H at the end of section 2d, some linguists merge syntactic and semantic levels, calling transitive subject 'agent' (abbreviated to 'A') and transitive object 'patient' (abbreviated to 'P'). This appears to be generalising upon the AFFECT semantic type (but substituting 'patient' for what I call Target). However, there are many other semantic types, and this approach misses out on the varied types of correspondences between syntactic functions and semantic roles, which are both subtle and significant.

4 Peripheral Arguments

The basics of an activity or state are provided by the core elements—predicate and core arguments. Additional (and optional) information may be added. For example: how it was done, for what purpose, the location, and the time. This can be achieved by attaching subordinate clauses (discussed in section 10) and by adjoining NPs expressing peripheral arguments. An example from English, which includes four peripheral arguments, is:

(1) [The hunter shot a deer]_{CORE}
     [for the king]   [with his longbow]   [in the forest]   [on Tuesday]
     BENEFACTIVE   INSTRUMENTAL   SPATIAL   TEMPORAL

4a *Marking of Peripheral Arguments*
A peripheral argument will—like a core argument—be realised by an NP. There has to be some grammatical marking to show that it is in peripheral (i.e. non-core) function and also what sort of information it conveys.

As we saw in section 2e, one way of distinguishing core arguments is through ordering. The language may have a convention that A comes before O, or vice versa; the predicate could be placed before, between, or after them.

(This could conceivably be extended to NPs in peripheral function—for example, a peripheral NP with a certain meaning could always immediately follow—or precede or come in the middle of—the core. But it is extremely rare for a peripheral NP to be marked solely by the position it occurs in.)

Every language has a wide range of peripheral arguments and each receives some grammatical marking. There are three alternatives: (i) by adpositions (as illustrated at (11–12) in section 2e for making core arguments in Japanese); or (ii) by case inflections; or (iii) by a combination of these.

(i) **Adpositions.** Languages which have no system of nominal case inflection follow this path. English is a prime example, as illustrated in (1). There are around four dozen prepositions. Most have a basic meaning, referring to space or time, with a number of extensions to more abstract senses. For example, the basic meaning of *on* relates to connection, as in *He sat on the chair*. But it is also used for time—*on Tuesday*—for mental attitude—*She dotes on her dogs*—for dependency—*He relies on his assistant*—and for state—*on parole*—among other things.

Japanese has about ten postpositions, used for marking core arguments—as in (11–12) of section 2e—and also all manner of peripheral arguments, as in:

(2) [John ga]$_S$ [Mary to] [kuruma de] [Kobe ni] it-ta$_{IPr}$
John NOM Mary WITH car BY Kobe TO go-PAST
John went to Kobe by car with Mary

(ii) **Case inflections.** Every noun in Dyirbal must make a choice from a system of nine cases. Core arguments are marked by absolutive (S and O functions, zero realisation) and ergative (A function, suffix *-ŋgu* with several allomorphic variants). These were illustrated by (15–16) in section 2e. Other cases, which mark peripheral arguments, are dative, instrumental, aversive, comitative, locative, allative, and ablative. For example:

(3) barrgan$_O$ yara-ŋgu$_A$ balga-n$_{TPr}$ waŋa-ru yalgay-ja
wallaby:ABS man-ERG hit-PAST boomerang-INSTR path-LOC
The man hit the wallaby with a boomerang on the path

The inflection *-ja* is used for locative in (3). The same suffixal form is used for the aversive case, which refers to something that the referent of the subject (S or A function) is scared of. Thus, with intransitive verb *ŋarba-* 'be frightened', we get:

(4) yara$_S$ ŋarba-n$_{IPr}$ walguy-ja
man:ABS be.frightened-PAST brown.snake-AVERSIVE
The man was frightened of the brown snake

Note that Dyirbal has no adpositions (prepositions or postpositions).
In some languages it is hard to decide whether a set of forms should be analysed as adpositions or as case affixes; indeed, they may have both functions, in different contexts.

(iii) **A combination of case inflections and adpositions.** Malayalam has a system of seven case inflections; each NP must make one choice from the system, depending on its function in the clause. Core functions are shown by nominative for S and A functions (zero realisation) and accusative for O function when the referent is animate (suffix -(y)e), as illustrated in (13–14) of section 2e.

Some peripheral arguments are marked just by a case inflection. For example, by dative case in (5) and by locative case in (6).

(5) kurtti-kə   amma$_A$ paal$_O$ korluttu$_{TPr}$
    child-DAT   mother   milk   give:PAST
    Mother gave milk to the child

(6) Joosaph$_S$ horttal-il   taamasikkunnu$_{IPr}$
    Joseph   hotel-LOC   stay:PRESENT
    Joseph stays in a hotel

Malayalam also has postpositions. Since every NP must select one term from the case system, each postposition follows an NP marked for a specific case. For instance, the NP preceding instrumental postposition *kornrtə* 'with' is in nominative case (with zero marking).

(7) kurtti$_A$ [katti   kornrtə]   kai$_O$ muriccu$_{TPr}$
    child   knife   INSTR   hand   cut:PAST
    The child cut its hand with a knife

And ablative postposition *ninnə* 'from' requires locative case on the NP it follows:

(8) [viirtt-il   ninnə]   aarum$_S$ vannilla$_{IPr}$
    house-LOC   ABLATIVE   anyone   come:PAST:NEGATIVE
    No one came from the house

Latin behaves in a similar way. Some peripheral arguments are marked just by a case ending. For instance, ablative cases is used for, among other senses, instrument, as in 'defend with javelins' and separation, in 'free from debt'. There are also about four dozen prepositions. Each must be followed by an NP in a specific case (we can recall, from section 2e, that in Latin all cases have non-zero realisation).

Many prepositions are used with the accusative case. For example:

ad 'to, towards'   *ante* 'before'   *inter* 'between, among'   *per* 'through'

Some are used with the ablative case, including:

a, ab 'by, from'   *cum* 'with'   *prō* 'before, on behalf of'   *sine* 'without'

And there are just a few prepositions with two possibilities. When used with the accusative they denote motion towards, and with the ablative case they denote rest. For example:

preposition	with accusative	with ablative
in	'into, onto, against'	'up to, along under'
sub	'in, on'	'under, underneath'

The head of an NP—whether in core or in peripheral function—is a lexeme, generally a noun. It can take lexical modifiers, typically adjectives. Individual languages may require a specification from a grammatical system, relating to the head of the NP; for example, gender, number, definiteness.

There must always be grammatical marking of the function of the NP in its clause—by an ordering convention, by an adposition, by choice from a system of case inflections, or by a combination of these means.

A peripheral noun phrase (NP) marked by a preposition, in a language such as English, is sometimes called a 'prepositional phrase'. The term is misleading. The head of the phrase *in the thick forest* is the same as the head of the plain NP *the thick forest*. The head is the lexeme *forest*. The preposition is simply an ancillary grammatical element. (One might as well use the term 'case phrase' for an NP whose syntactic function is marked by a case, such as *yalgay-ja* 'on the path' in (3) from Dyirbal and *horttal-il* 'in a hotel', in (6) from Malayalam.)

L   There is a long-standing habit of saying that, when an NP is marked by an adposition, the main part of the phrase is the 'object' of the adposition. In relation to *in the thick forest*, followers of this approach would say that *the thick forest* is the 'prepositional object' of *in*. This is putting the cart before the horse. The very name 'pre-position' states that this is a grammatical marker which is positioned before the NP; it is the NP that has reference, and which indicates what is being talked about. A transitive predicate, the lexical centre of its clause, does take an object; it is confusing to then say that a preposition, a marker of syntactic function, also 'takes an object'.

M The term 'govern' is sometimes used to describe the relation between a predicate and a core argument. For instance one may say that, in Latin, a transitive predicate 'governs' an object in accusative case. This cannot be objected to—a predicate does determine what core arguments are required in its clause, and their function will be marked by the appropriate case.

But the term 'govern' is then sometimes extended in a quite inappropriate way. Again in Latin, the preposition *cum* 'with' may be said to 'govern ablative case'. The more appropriate description is: 'a comitative peripheral argument in Latin is marked by a combination of preposition *cum* and ablative case on the head noun of the NP and its modifiers'. Marking the function of the NP is shown by the interlinking of preposition and case; neither has priority over the other.

To say that 'a preposition governs a case', indicating that these two grammatical elements co-occur, is to assign a quite different meaning to *govern* from that which it has in 'an intransitive predicate governs an S core argument', meaning that one lexical constituent requires another lexical constituent to complete a clause as a meaningful proposition.

N Quite recently, there has arisen the eccentric idea of taking a preposition to be the 'head' of a phrase for which it marks syntactic function. This is confusing lexicon and grammar. The central meaning in any portion of language is carried by lexemes. Grammatical elements provide ancillary semantic information, mark syntactic function, and link together clauses into sentences.

If a preposition is regarded as phrasal head in a language which shows syntactic function by prepositions, then a case affix should surely be regarded a phrasal head in a language which marks syntactic function by case inflection. For *horttal-il* 'in a hotel', in (6) from Malayalam, we would have to take suffix *-il* as head of the phrase. The case system for this—and many other languages—includes one term with zero realisation. Consider *amma-∅* 'mother' in A function, from (5) in Malayalam, where ∅ indicates that nominative case has zero realisation. Presumably, the zero element, ∅, should be taken as head of the phrase.

There must always be some way of showing the syntactic function of an NP. In a number of languages, including English, core functions are shown by ordering; in *The big bear chased the little boy*, the fact that *the big bear* is in A function is shown by its relative position before *the little boy*, which is in O function. To be consistent we would have to say that 'coming before O argument' is head of the phrase *the big bear* in this clause. (Well, nonsense does spawn further nonsense.)

4b *Meaning of Peripheral Arguments*

We focus here on English (in fact the analysis does apply, in large part, to many other languages).

I   Spatial and Temporal Peripheral Arguments

The first point to note is that all but a handful of the four dozen or so prepositions have a basic meaning referring to space or time or both. These can be roughly categorised:

- *Basic meaning spatial*: (a) also relating to time; for example *at, on, in, to, from*; (b) with no temporal sense; for example, *among, beside(s), beneath, despite*.
- *Basic meaning temporal*: (a) also relating to space: *before, after, past*; (b) with no spatial sense: *since, till/until, during*.

The previous section discussed eight semantic types involving transitive verbs. Two other semantic types, which include many intransitive verbs, are:

The MOTION type, all with semantic role 'Moving (thing)'. Most members are intransitive with the Moving role as S argument; they include: *run, walk, march, jump, arrive, go, come*.

The REST type, all with semantic role 'Resting (thing)'. Many members are intransitive with the Resting role as S argument; they include: *sit, stand, crouch, kneel, float*.

There are two varieties of peripheral arguments marked by a preposition with spatial or temporal sense:

  (a) Inner peripherals . These provide spatial modification of the predicate; the meaning of the preposition is keyed to the meaning of the verb which heads the VP in predicate slot. Spatial specification can relate to either motion or location.

- *Peripheral arguments relating to motion may be used with verbs of motion*. For example:

(9)   The doctor walked [from the hospital] [along the river] [to his house]

- *Peripheral arguments relating to location may be used with verbs of rest*. For example:

(10) My daughter stood [on the bench] [in the garden] [at the vicarage]

4B MEANING OF PERIPHERAL ARGUMENTS

Inner peripherals are semantically integrated with the predicate. A verb of motion or rest can be used on its own, with just an S argument, but there is the expectation of a peripheral argument specifying the locus of the motion or the rest.

(b) Outer peripherals. Most types of activity are situated in some place and at some time. This can be specified by peripheral arguments stating spatial setting and/or temporal location (but not those indicating motion). Unlike inner peripherals, there is no association between the meaning of the preposition and that of the predicate. In effect, virtually any outer peripheral can modify virtually any core clause.

We can select some descriptions of happenings, chosen pretty well at random:

Jim cut his finger	Tom vomited	The police arrested the criminal
Jane insulted the teacher	Kate took a photo	The old man enjoyed the dancing

To these core clauses (and an indefinite number more) can be added one or more outer peripherals stating location and/or time, such as:

[in the garden]   [at the museum]   [after lunch]   [on Tuesday]

The complete clause must be plausible but, unlike with inner peripherals, there is no particular association between the meaning of the preposition and the meaning of the verb.

II   Other Types of Peripheral Arguments

Peripheral arguments which do not relate to space and time include (there are quite a few more):
(a)   Instrumental—hit with a stick, eat with knife and fork, cover with a cloth
(b)   Accompaniment—walk with the dog, crawling with insects, lives with his mother
(c)   Benefactive—write a letter for Jason, testify in court for his friend
(d)   Purpose—plan for the future, prepare for the worst, store for the winter
(e)   Topic—talk of the weather, brag of one's success, repent of the crime
(f)   Means—lead by the hand, travel by train, do it by trickery
(g)   Source—die from cancer, benefit from the change, evolve from an amoeba

The few prepositions in English which do not have spatial or temporal senses play a large role here—*with* in (a–b), *for* in (c–d), and *of* in (e). *By* has a rather limited spatial sense (*He walked by the church*) and is used predominantly to mark non-spatial peripherals, as in (f). And many of the spatial prepositions do have additional senses, such as *from* in (g).

Many languages have an 'applicative' syntactic derivation which takes a peripheral argument and places it in O function. The scope of the applicative—that is, which kinds of peripheral arguments it applies to—varies from language to language. But surveying the derivation cross-linguistically, each of the peripheral types (a–g) may be placed in O function in one language or another.

4c *Extended Intransitive and Extended Transitive Clause Types*

All languages have plain intransitive and plain transitive clause types. In some there are variants on these, which can be called 'extended intransitive' and 'extended transitive'. Each has an additional argument, the 'extension' (E) added to the core. That is:

CLAUSE TYPE/PREDICATE		CORE ARGUMENTS		
(a)	intransitive	S		
(b)	extended intransitive	S		E
(c)	transitive	A	O	
(d)	extended transitive	A	O	E

Both (b) and (c) have two core arguments, but they are of a quite different nature. Argument S in (b) has the same grammatical properties as S in (a), quite different from those of A in (c–d). And argument E in (b) has the same grammatical properties as E in (d), quite different from those of O in (c–d).

This can be illustrated from Tongan, which belongs to the Polynesian branch of the Austronesian family. Tongan shows an absolutive/ergative scheme, and marks syntactic function by prepositions. Thus (' is a glottal stop):

PREPOSITION	FORM	MARKS ARGUMENTS
absolutive (ABS)	'a	S, O
ergative (ERG)	'e	A
dative (DAT)	ki	E

4C EXTENDED INTRANSITIVE AND EXTENDED TRANSITIVE CLAUSE TYPES

Example sentences are (where ART indicates 'article'):

(11a) intransitive [na'e 'alu] ['a e fefiné]$_S$
 PAST go ABS ART woman
 The woman (S) went

(11b) extended [na'e sio] ['a e fefiné]$_S$ [ki he tangatá]$_E$
 intransitive PAST see ABS ART woman DAT ART man
 The woman (S) saw the man (E)

(11c) transitive [na'e taa'i] ['a e tangatá]$_O$ ['e he fefiné]$_A$
 PAST hit ABS ART man ERG ART woman
 The woman (A) hit the man (O)

(11d) extended [na'e 'oange] ['a e tohi]$_O$ ['e he fefiné]$_A$
 transitive PAST give ABS ART book ERG ART woman
 [ki he tangatá]
 DAT ART man
 The woman (A) gave a book (O) to the man (E)

Note that NPs may occur in any order after the predicate, their functions being shown by the prepositions.

Whereas absolutive 'a and ergative 'e just mark core arguments, dative ki is basically the marker for a peripheral argument (covering 'to', 'until', and 'about') and has the secondary function of marking the additional core argument of extended intransitive and extended transitive clause types.

A number of semantic types of transitive verbs were illustrated for English in section 3. In Tongan, verbs from the ATTENTION and LIKING types occur in extended intransitive clauses, the remainder in transitive clauses. We thus get the following associations of semantic roles with syntactic functions S and E in an extended intransitive clause, and with A and O in a transitive clause:

Semantic type	Roles as S argument	Roles as E argument
ATTENTION	Perceiver	Impression
LIKING	Experiencer	Stimulus

Semantic type	Roles as A argument	Roles as O argument
AFFECT	Agent	Target
THINKING	Cogitator	Thought

Why should verbal concepts which are all coded in the same way—as transitive verbs—in English and other languages, be divided up in this way? There is a semantic reason for it.

The criterion we employed for an NP to be in A function was that its referent has 'the potential to initiate or control the activity or state'. In the course of the discussion of types—one-by-one—in section 3, this criterion was seen to be amply satisfied for the Agent, Cogitator, Decision-Maker, and Speaker semantic roles. But for the Perceiver role from the ATTENTION type, and also for the Experiencer role from the LIKING type, the criterion was satisfied only rather weakly. Verbs in these types do have two core arguments, but it is problematic whether one of them has sufficient potential to instigate or control the activity (or state) involved, such that it should be associated with A syntactic function. As a result, in Tongan—and a number of similar languages—Perceiver and Experiencer are linked to S (rather than to A) syntactic function, and a new core argument slot, E, is introduced to accommodate the other core role.

Other languages have different ways of indicating that Perceiver and Experiencer only partially satisfy the criterion to be A argument. The North-east Caucasian language Avar basically follows the absolutive/ergative scheme. But while ergative case is generally used for an NP in A function, verbs in the LIKING type have a dative A, and A is marked as locative for ATTENTION verbs.

Just a few languages are like Tongan in having a special 'extended intransitive' clause type. In contrast, the 'extended transitive' clause type (often called 'ditransitive') is found in very many—although by no means in all—languages. It includes 'give' and usually just a small number of other verbs. There is competition between semantic roles Gift and Recipient as to which is to be associated with the O role. Typically, there may be two construction types, one for each possibility with the role that is unsuccessful bearing peripheral marking.

(This was illustrated for English by (1–2) in section 3. Here we have the unusual situation that when Recipient is in O function, the Gift NP just follows it, with no marking.)

5 Clauses within Phrases and Clauses within Clauses

In section 2i a diagram was presented showing three 'storeys' in language structure—words functioning in phrases, which in turn function within clauses. There are in fact two extra types of connection within the edifice:
- A *relative clause* (RC) functions, like an adjective, as a type of modifier to the head lexeme of an NP.
- A *complement clause* (CoCl) functions, instead of an NP, in a core argument slot of a clause.

These two varieties of subordinate clause may look alike at a casual glance. For example, the following two sentences would look similar if one ignored the labelled constituency brackets:

(1) [The policeman]$_{NP:A}$ knows$_{VP:TPr}$ [the dog [that chased the cat]$_{RC}$]$_{NP:O}$
(2) [The policeman]$_{NP:A}$ knows$_{VP:TPr}$ [that the dog chased the cat]$_{CoCl:O}$

These two single-clause sentences have totally different structures and meanings. In (1), *that chased the cat* is a relative clause to *the dog*, helping to identify which dog it is. The sentence could be rephrased as:

(3) The policeman is acquainted with the dog which chased the cat

In (2) *that the dog chased the cat* is complement clause functioning as O argument for the transitive verb *know*. It could be rephrased as:

(4) The policeman is aware of the fact that the dog chased the cat

In every language, we are likely often to encounter one word taking on several quite different tasks. For English, *that* is a 'relative pronoun' in (1), serving to introduce the RC; an alternative would be *which*, as in (3). In (2), *that* introduces one type of complement clause; *that* could be omitted from (2). (*That* could not be omitted from (1) with the sentence still being recognised as including a relative clause. If *that* were to be omitted from (1), the sentence could only be interpreted as the complement clause construction (2) with its *that* omitted.) A third use of *that* is as a demonstrative modifier within an NP, as in *that dog*. And its fourth use is as a deictic comprising the whole of an NP, as when someone says *I don't like that*, at the same time pointing at some rebarbative foodstuff.

We can now discuss these two kinds of subordinate clause, one at a time.

5a   Relative Clauses

A relative clause (RC) construction involves two full clauses which share a common argument (CA). Either clause can be taken as the main clause with the other clause being an RC functioning as a modifier to the occurrence of the CA in the main clause.

Almost every language has a relative clause construction. The meaning is constant and straightforward—the RC assists in identifying the referent of the CA. On hearing *The bishop is ill* one might not know which bishop was being spoken of. The reference of *the bishop* can be restricted (and often uniquely identified) by adding an RC:

(5) The bishop who lives in Caracas is ill

There are many bishops but adding a 'restrictive relative clause', limits the reference. In some—but by no means all—languages there is also a 'non-restrictive relative clause', as illustrated by:

(6) The Pope, who lives in Rome, is ill

The Pope already has a unique referent so that in this case the RC simply provides non-restricting information. Restrictive and non-restrictive RCs have the same form; they are distinguished by the fact that non-restrictive RCs employ appositional intonation, shown by commas in (6).

Languages differ in the grammatical possibilities they allow with respect to the CA. There may be limitations on what function the CA may have in the main clause and/or in the RC. The CA may be stated just in the main clause, or just in the RC, or in both.

In English the CA can be in virtually any function in both main clause and RC. It is stated in the main clause, and in the RC the CA is replaced by a relative pronoun—*which*, or *that*, or *who* or *whom*; or *where* for place, or *when* for time. This relative pronoun then moves to the beginning of the clause.

Consider underlying clauses:

(7) The doctor saw the lion
(8) The lion bit the tourist

(7) and (8) share a CA, *the lion*. We can take either of them as main clause and the other as RC:

(9) [The doctor]_A saw [the lion [which_A bit the [tourist]_O]_RC]_O
(10) [The lion] [(which_O) [[the doctor]_A saw]_RC]_A [bit the tourist]_O

Relative pronoun *which* in (9) and (10) replaces CA *the lion* within the RC. In (10) *the lion* was in O function and its replacement, *which*, is initial within the RC. The *which* can be omitted—the RC is transitive (from its verb *see*), the A argument (*the doctor*) is stated, the O argument is not stated in its normal position immediately after the predicate and so it must be this which is relativised. This is clear whether or not the substitute *which* is included, and thus *which* could be omitted without affecting the meaning.

In (9) the CA was in A function, in clause-initial position, and so the relative pronoun *which* just replaces it. The *which* in (9) cannot be omitted simply because there is a rule of English grammar that a predicate must be preceded by an NP (in S or A function); it is *the lion* in (8) and *which* in the RC of (9) that satisfy this condition.

Languages differ in the syntactic organisation of relative clause constructions, but the semantic effect is much the same.

5b *Complement Clauses*

Many—but not all—languages have a set of complement clauses (CoCl's) which can fill a core argument slot as an alternative to an NP. An example from English is:

(11) [The teacher]_{NP:A} believes_{VP:TPr} John_{NP:O}
(12) [The teacher]_{NP:A} believes_{VP:TPr} [that John is telling the truth]_{CoCl:O}

There can be a number of different kinds of complement clause constructions, each with a different meaning. Three main varieties may be recognised for English, here described rather briefly.

I   A THAT clause

The CoCl has the structure of a main clause, simply preceded by complementiser *that*. It refers to the fact that something took place, as in (2) and:

(13) I know [(that) Tim won the race yesterday]

There is an interrogative variant of the THAT CoCl, with the *that* replaced by *whether* (or *if*): *I don't know* [*whether Tim won the race yesterday*]. Or the doubt may focus on a core argument, *I don't know* [*who won the race yesterday*] or on a place, or on a time, *I don't know [when Tim won the race]*. Note that complementiser *that* may be omitted from (13)—as from (2)—without any loss of meaning. However a WH- complementiser (*whether, who, when, where*) may not be omitted.

II   An ING Clause

The VP is not marked for tense, instead the first word of the VP takes suffix *-ing*. The subject (A or S) NP of an ING CoCl may take suffix *-'s*, although it is quite often omitted. This type of CoCl refers to something extended in time, often noting the way in which it unfolds. For example, after listening to the radio commentary on a football game, one might say:

(14)   I heard [New Zealand('s) beat-ing France]

In contrast, a THAT clause would just report a fact:

(15)   I heard [that New Zealand beat France]

Substituting an NP for the CoCl, (15) would become *I heard the result* whereas (14) would become *I heard the game* (that is, every detail of it).

III   A (FOR) TO Clause

The VP is again not marked for tense; complementiser *for* comes at the beginning of the CoCl and *to* is placed before the VP. This type of CoCl describes the intention of the referent of the subject of the main clause that the activity which is referred to by the CoCl should happen. For example:

(16)   I'm planning [for Jose to organise the event]

This has similar meaning to a THAT CoCl whose VP includes a modal modifier (*should, could, would, will*, etc.). Corresponding to (16) there could be:

(17)   I'm planning [that Jose should organise the event]

The subject of a (FOR) TO CoCl will be omitted (plus the preceding *for*) when it is identical with the subject of the main clause. Rather than **I'm planning [for me to organise the event]*, one would say:

(18)   I'm planning [to organise the event]

5B COMPLEMENT CLAUSES 39

Note that no such omission is possible from a THAT CoCl. One would have to say *I'm planning* [*that I should organise the event*].

Different kinds of CoCl show different pragmatic possibilities. Compare:

(19) When he woke up on Wednesday, Simon decided [that he was sick]
(20) When he woke up on Wednesday, Simon decided [to be sick]

Sentence (19) describes a fact—Simon woke with a fever and realised that he was truly sick. In contrast, (20) puts forward an intention—Simon wanted to attend the football match and made up his mind to put on a pretence and tell his workplace that he was sick.

A CoCl fills a core slot in clause structure as an alternative to an NP. It must be noted that a CoCl is quite different from an NP. Compare the NP in O function in (21) with the ING CoCl in O function in (22).

(21) Fred$_{NP:A}$ saw$_{VP:TPr}$ [Mary's careful painting$_{NOUN:HEAD}$ of the bridge]$_{NP:O}$
(22) Fred$_{NP:A}$ saw$_{VP:TPr}$ [Mary('s)$_{NP:A}$ carefully paint-ing$_{VP:TPr}$ [the bridge]$_{NP:O}$]$_{CoCl:O}$

In (21), *painting* is a noun, head of its NP. It is modified by possessor *Mary's*, adjective *careful*, and post-head modifier *of the bridge*. In (22) *paint* is a verb with *Mary* as its A argument and *the bridge* as its O argument; suffix *-ing* on *paint* and optional *'s* on Mary mark it as an ING CoCl.

Note three important differences. First, *the bridge* is in O function in (22) and takes no preposition whereas in (21) *the bridge* is part of a modifying phrase *of the bridge*. The noun *painting* takes adjective *careful* as modifier in (21) whereas verb *paint* takes adverb *carefully* as modifier in (22). And the possessive suffix *-'s* is obligatory on *Mary* in (21) but CoCl marker *'s* may be omitted from (22).

The meanings of the two sentences are quite different. In (21) Fred saw the completed picture, whereas in (22) he watched Mary while she was creating it.

O   Naive approaches to analysis which use formulas 'Sentence → NP (i.e. in A or S function) + VP', and then 'VP → V (+ NP (i.e. in O function))' deal with the fact that a complement clause can be in O function by saying that a CoCl is essentially an NP. Consideration of (21) and (22) shows the inadequacy of such an approach.

There can be all manner of recursion—an RC within an RC, a CoCl within a CoCl, an RC within a CoCl, and a CoCl within an RC. A somewhat extreme example is:

(23) John saw [that the criminal [who had planned [to kidnap the heiress [who loves singing songs [which her grandmother had taught her]$_{RC}$]$_{CoCl}$]$_{RC}$]$_{RC}$ hoped [to evade the detective [who never failed [to catch people [who were too confident]$_{RC}$]$_{CoCl}$]$_{RC}$]$_{CoCl}$]$_{CoCl}$

This is less difficult to parse when spoken than when written (because of the role of intonation). Nevertheless, recursion of this type is a possible resource which is utilised rather sparingly in everyday use of language.

P Latin was the language of prestige when scholars began to write grammars of English, and English was treated as if it were a variant of Latin. Terms from Latin grammar were taken over even if there was not really anything corresponding in English. A pervasive example of this is 'infinitive'.

In Latin, 'infinitive' was used for the form of a verb which—unlike the verb form in a main clause—was not marked for the person and number of a subject, but did show tense. This was a nominalisation, which functioned as an indeclinable neuter noun, that could function as head of an NP.

On the basis of partial translation equivalence, early Latin-orientated grammars of English used 'infinitive' for preposition *to* plus the root form of a verb, and this terminology persists very strongly today. In a (FOR) TO complement clause construction, such as *John wanted to demolish the building*, the sequence *to demolish* is said to be an infinitive. In fact these two words do not form a constituent; for example, an adverb can be inserted between them—*John wanted to completely demolish the building*. (Latin-oriented prescriptivists forbid such 'split infinitives'. However, *John wanted completely to demolish the building* sounds infelicitous and in any case it has a rather different meaning.)

Then the form without *to*, here *demolish*, came to be called the 'bare infinitive'. But an infinitive in Latin was a nominalisation which had some of the syntactic possibilities of a noun. The verb root *demolish* is not a nominalisation; it cannot be preceded by an article (the nominalisation of this verb is *demolition*).

Unfortunately, the term 'infinitive' is firmly entrenched in grammatical studies of English and other European languages. Sensibly, it is generally avoided in recent comprehensive studies of languages from other parts of the world.

5C *Complement Clauses and Semantic Roles*

The use of complement clauses is semantically determined. There must be a compatibility of meaning between a complement clause and the verb it is used with. Or, to be more precise, the semantic role with which it is associated. This can be illustrated for English.

For the verbs in some semantic types, each core argument slot must be filled by an NP, and not by a CoCl (except perhaps when a verb is used in a highly metaphorical sense). This applies for the AFFECT and GIVING types (discussed in section 3) and also to MOTION, REST and CORPOREAL (including *eat*, *cough*, *bleed*, *laugh*, and so on), among other semantic types.

Generally, a CoCl will not appear in a peripheral argument, nor in a semantic role which is linked to A (or S) syntactic function. Consider the four semantic types THINKING, DECIDING, ATTENTION, and SPEAKING, discussed in section 3. The Cogitator, Decision-Maker, Perceiver, and Speaker semantic roles—which relate to the transitive subject, A, core argument—will invariably be filled by NPs. It is the non-A roles which may be expressed by either an NP or a CoCl—Thought, Course, Impression, and Message.

All verbs in the THINKING type may have a THAT CoCl in the Thought role, describing a fact. They include *know*—in (2) and (13)—*believe*—in (12)—*assume*, *suppose*, *realise*, and *infer*. Some may also relate to an unfolding activity and then take an ING CoCl; for example, *imagine* and *contemplate*. Just a few, including *remember*, may also describe a potentiality, with a (FOR) TO CoCl. *Remember* refers to a fact, with a THAT CoCl in (24), to an activity, with an ING CoCl in (25), and to the need to satisfy a potentiality, with a (FOR) TO CoCl in (26).

(24) Gerald remembered [that he had read *Candide*]
(he knew for a fact he had done it, but couldn't recall anything of the plot)

(25) Gerald remembered [reading *Candide*]
(and could recall every detail of the story)

(26) Gerald remembered [to read *Candide*]
(it had to be completed before the exam)

In the DECIDING semantic type, there are varied possibilities for a CoCl in the Course role. *Decide on* may occur with all the types. An ING CoCl is used to describe an activity in *The gardener decided on [pruning the roses today]*.

A THAT CoCl, describing a fact, is in (19) and a (FOR) TO CoCl, demonstrating an intention, is in (20). Note that a preposition, such as the *on* in *decide on*, is always omitted before a *that*, *for*, or *to* complementiser. *Plan* occurs with THAT and (FOR) TO clauses in (16–18) and (23).

Choose may take THAT and (FOR) TO—but not ING—CoCl's. For example *I chose [that we should take our vacation in Spain this year]* and *We chose [(for) Rev. Egbert to deliver the sermon]*. However, hyponyms of *choose*—such as *select*, *pick (out)*, and *appoint*—must have a concrete referent for the Course role, realised by an NP and not by a CoCl.

A fair number of verbs from the ATTENTION type may have in the Impression role either a THAT CoCl, for becoming aware of a fact, or an ING CoCl, for witnessing an activity. This was illustrated for *see* in (23) and (22) and for *hear* in (15) and (14). Others include *observe*, *show*, and *witness*. *Recognise* and *discover* are restricted to THAT clauses. And the Impression role may only be an NP, not a CoCl, for *investigate*, *scrutinise*, and *explore*.

The SPEAKING semantic type includes a wide array of verbs for all of which the Speaker semantic role relates to A syntactic function. There are a number of possibilities for a CoCl in Message role, according to the subtype of verbs involved. One may *describe* an activity, with an ING CoCl, *discuss* or *mention* a piece of news, with a THAT CoCl, *propose* or *offer* that something should be done, with a (FOR) TO CoCl, and much more besides.

For the LIKING semantic type, the Experiencer semantic role, which relates to syntactic function A, can only be an NP. But the Stimulus role, in O function, may describe fact, activity or potentiality, with appropriate choice of CoCl. This can be illustrated with *like*:

(27) Father likes it [that Mary plays the piano]
    (he considers that all young ladies should have this skill)

(28) Father likes [Mary('s) playing the piano]
    (he delights in listening to her play)

(29) Father would like [(for) Mary to play the piano]
    (but she absolutely refuses to fulfil this potentiality)

Those LIKING verbs with the widest range of meaning take all three types of CoCl—*like*, *love*, *prefer*, and *hate*. Others have a narrower scope which limits their CoCl possibilities. For example, *dislike*, *loathe*, and *enjoy* just take the ING and THAT varieties, while *detest* is pretty well restricted to an ING CoCl.

5C COMPLEMENT CLAUSES AND SEMANTIC ROLES

A fascinating feature of English is that the ANNOYING semantic type has the same semantic roles as the LIKING type, but reverses their links to syntactic functions. The Experiencer, which may only be realised by an NP, is now in O function, and the Stimulus role, which can be a CoCl, is in A function. This is a rare instance of a CoCl satisfying the criterion for A function, 'being responsible for the state'.

Parallel to the three kinds of CoCl in O function with *like*, in (27–9), there can be the three kinds in A function with *annoy*:

(30) [That Mary plays the piano] annoys Father
(he thinks this is an indulgence, and that she should study more instead)

(31) [Mary('s) playing the piano] annoys father
(he can't stand the noise)

(32) [For Mary to play the piano] would annoy father
(if you want to make him really angry, just suggest this)

In place of *annoy* in (30–2) we could use *please, anger, impress, worry, disgust, amuse*, or other verbs from the ANNOYING semantic type.

It is unusual in English to have a CoCl in sentence-initial position. This only happens, in the main, with verbs from the ANNOYING type. In fact, the language minimises this by typically extraposing a THAT or a (FOR) TO CoCl to the end of the sentence, and substituting *it* for the CoCl in the position before the predicate:

(30') It annoys Father [that Mary plays the piano]
(32') It would annoy father [for Mary to play the piano]

Note that an ING CoCl in A function does not extrapose. (The reason for this is a matter for speculation.)

The meaning of a verb motivates the varieties of CoCl it can be used with. For instance, *fail* describes 'being unable to gain some goal' and is limited to a (FOR) TO CoCl, as in (23). Note that only a sample of the Semantic types involving CoCl's has been surveyed here; others include the BEGINNING, WANTING, MAKING, and HELPING types.

A scattering of verbs, which in their basic meaning require core arguments to be filled just by NPs may take a CoCl in A function when used in a metaphorical sense. For example, an extended activity—described by an ING CoCl—might be described as *eating* time. Thus:

(33) [The Dean's slowly reading out all the proposals] has eaten into the time available for discussion

And *give* can be extended to the provision of social backing, with the Donor role then being a THAT CoCl, as in:

(34) [That the Dean supports the proposal] gives it a greater chance of success

5d   *Conclusion*

Some languages have more types of CoCl than English—for example, there may be two 'potential' varieties, for direct and indirect intention/will. And some have less—one CoCl type may be employed for both 'fact' and 'activity'. Generally, the occurrence of kinds of CoCl with non-A roles in semantic types is fairly similar to that in English.

There can, however, be considerable differences. There is just one kind of CoCl in Jarawara (from the small Arawá family, spoken deep in the Amazonian jungle), covering both activity and purpose. It is used in O syntactic function for verbs of THINKING, ATTENTION, and LIKING. But its most common employment is as S argument for intransitive verbs, including those referring to motion and rest. For instance what would be said in English as *I am standing holding a plate* would be in Jarawara, literally '[My holding a plate]$_{CoCl:S}$ stands$_{IPr}$'.

Jarawara has intransitive verbs describing states, which would be rendered by adjectives in English, for instance *amosa-* 'be good'. These typically have a CoCl as S argument, as in:

(35) [tika$_S$ hijar-i]$_{CoCl:S}$ [amosa-tee   ama
     2sg   talk-COMPLEMENTISER   be.good-HABITUAL   EXTENDED
     ti-ke]$_{IPr}$
     2sg-DEC
     You always talk well (lit. Your talking is always good)

The CoCl is here marked by *-i* replacing the final *-a* of the verb. (The grammar of Jarawara is complex. In (35) the 2sg in S function within the complement clause, which is itself in S function within the main clause, is repeated as 2sg prefix *ti-* before the declarative suffix within the main clause predicate.)

Quite a few languages do not have complement clause constructions per se. They achieve similar means by extended use of other construction types (including relative clauses) as 'complementation strategies'.

6   Free and Bound Pronouns

6a   *The Heterogeneous Class of Pronouns*

'Pronoun' is used as a cover term for two quite different phenomena, which should be carefully distinguished.

(a) Speech act participants. If Moira and William were in a room together, and William expressed gratitude towards Moira. William *could* describe what has happened by saying:

(1)   William thanked Moira

However, there is an alternative. Every known language has what are called a '1st person pronoun', referring to the speaker, and a '2nd person pronoun', referring to the addressee. Rather than (1), William would say:

(2)   I thanked you

I and *you* have unique reference, to the two participants in this speech act—*I* for the person who is speaking, and *you* for the person who is being spoken to.

(b) Anaphoric elements. Let us now look at sentences referring to people other than speaker and addressee. Whereas *I thanked you* is totally specified, if one heard *He thanked her*, it would not be possible to know who was being talked about. Some context is needed; for example:

(3)   William and Moira came into the room and he thanked her

Since *William* is generally a male name and *Moira* is generally a female name, one would infer that the masculine anaphoric element *he* relates to William and the feminine anaphoric element *her* relates to Moira—that is, William thanked Moira.

So far, so good. But what happens if the two people involved are of the same sex, as in:

(4) William and Thomas came into the room and he thanked him

Here we can't tell who did the thanking. *He* could relate to William and *him* to Thomas, or vice versa. It can be seen that the information coded in anaphoric elements is limited.

The term 'pronoun', used for 1st and 2nd persons, is conventionally extended to also apply to these anaphoric elements, labelling them '3rd person pronouns'. But whereas 1st and 2nd person pronouns have unique reference to speech act participants, '3rd person pronouns' have no explicit reference at all; they are in most cases just a shorthand for referring back to NPs with definite reference.

Modern linguistics has firm foundations in early work on classical languages. One can understand how the term '3rd person pronoun' came into use from the neat paradigms in these languages for verbal inflection. This can be illustrated from Latin, for verb *ven-* 'come'—see (17) in section 2e—in present tense, active voice, indicative mood:

(5) | 1sg | ven-iō | 'I come' | 1pl | ven-īmus | 'we come' |
     | 2sg | ven-īs | 'you (sg) come' | 2pl | ven-ītis | 'you (pl) come' |
     | 3sg | ven-it | 'she/he comes' | 3pl | ven-iunt | 'they come' |

Identification of subject (S or A function) is shown by 'bound pronouns', fused with information on tense, voice, and mood.

The neatness of this paradigm is entirely superficial. A word from the top two rows can make up a complete utterance with fully specified reference—*ven-iō* 'I (the speaker) come', and so on. This does not apply for the third row. 'She/he' is non-specific; it refers to a person who is likely to be identified through an NP; for instance *Servus venit* 'The slave he.comes'. (Alternatively, its reference could be made clear by pointing to a person other than speaker or addressee: *He comes*, pointing a finger at Tom.)

The easy—and naive—approach is just to analyse the surface patterns of a language. But in order to understand how a language really works one needs to dig down in order to uncover the underlying syntactic structures and their semantic correlates. These will be more-or-less disorderly. But they may be coded by the grammar into neat surface arrays, as in the Latin paradigm just given.

If modern linguistics had been spawned, not around the olden-days shores of the Mediterranean but in the rainforest of north-east Queensland, it would have a quite different face. Dyirbal does have 1st and 2nd person pronouns,

6A THE HETEROGENEOUS CLASS OF PRONOUNS

like every other language, and it combines them with singular, dual and plural number specification:

| 1sg | ŋaja | 1du | ŋali | 1pl | ŋana |
| 2sg | ŋinda | 2du | ñubala | 2pl | ñurra |

However, there is no corresponding array of '3rd person' pronouns. (Many other languages, scattered across the world, are like Dyirbal in this respect.)

Every language has 1st and 2nd person pronouns, relating to speech act participants. However, only some languages have forms which pattern in a similar way and refer to non-speech-act-participants.

How then, one might then ask, does a language like Dyirbal deal with anaphora, like that handled in English by 3rd person pronouns *he* and *she* in a sentence like (3)? By a quite different grammatical means. (And other languages lacking a '3rd person' in their pronoun paradigm use different means again.)

Dyirbal has four genders and each noun is typically accompanied by a 'marker' which shows its gender, and also the case appropriate to its syntactic function, plus whether its reference is 'there' (initial *ba-*), 'here' (initial *ya-*), or 'not visible' (initial *ŋa-*). The gender markers can accompany a noun, and they can also be used on their own as anaphoric elements. Consider the sentence:

(6) [bayi   ŋuma]$_S$ mayi-n   [bala-n-ambila
    THERE.ABS.I father:ABS   come.in-PAST   THERE.ABS-II-COMIT
    yabu-bila];   bala-n$_S$ wurrba-ñu
    mother-COMIT THERE.ABS-II   speak-PAST
    Father came in with mother; she spoke

Bayi is the marker for gender I (including masculine humans), here in absolutive case accompanying *ŋuma* 'father', which is the head of the NP in S function for intransitive verb *mayin* 'came in'. Noun *yabu* 'mother' takes marker *balan* for gender II (which includes feminine humans). Both *balan* and *yabu* take comitative suffix *-(am)bile* 'with' indicating that *balan-ambila yabu-bila* 'with mother' is a comitative peripheral NP.

The second clause, with intransitive verb *wurrbañu* 'spoke' has *balan* as its S argument. This is an anaphoric element referring back to *balan yabu* 'mother', showing that it was mother who spoke. If it had been father who spoke, the second clause would be *bayi wurrbañu*.

In summary, languages have diverse means for showing anaphora, often quite different from the ways of indicating who is speaker and who is addressee within a context of direct speech.

6b Pronouns and Nouns

NPs fill core and peripheral argument slots in a clause. There are several possibilities for the head of an NP.
- The head may be a noun and this may, optionally, be modified by adjectives, demonstratives, relative clauses, etc.
- The head may be a 1st or 2nd person pronoun (or a '3rd person' pronoun in languages which have these). Languages vary as to whether a pronoun as head may take modifiers, relative clauses, and so on.

Section 2e explained the alternative schemes for indicating core arguments—accusative, with S marked like A, and ergative, with S marked like O. In some languages all NPs follow the same scheme. But in others noun-headed and pronoun-headed NPs differ, one employing the ergative and the other the accusative scheme. There was exemplification in section 2e of the absolutive/ergative case system for nouns (and adjectives) in Dyirbal. In this language 1st and 2nd person pronouns differ, being on a nominative/accusative basis. The overall system may be outlined, with a sample member for each word class:

Cases	1st and 2nd person pronouns e.g. 1st dual	Syntactic function	Gender markers e.g. gender II	Nouns e.g. 'dog'	Cases
NOMINATIVE ŋali (zero suffix)		A	ba-ŋgu-n	guda-ŋgu	ERGATIVE (suffix -ŋgu)
		S	bala-n	guda	ABSOLUTIVE (zero suffix)
ACCUSATIVE ŋali-na (suffix -na)		O			

It was noted in the previous section that Dyirbal has nothing which could be identified as '3rd person pronouns'; in place of these, anaphoric reference is shown by gender markers. The table includes the marker (referring to 'there' with initial ba(la)-) for gender II. Onto the root ba(la)- is added ergative suffix -*ŋgu* for A function, or zero (showing absolutive case) for S and O functions. The ending -*n* marks gender II.

The point to note is that the gender markers—although fulfilling a function similar to 3rd person pronouns in other languages—inflect on an ergative scheme, like nouns (and adjectives), which differs from the accusative scheme for 1st and 2nd person pronouns.

A wide variety of languages show a split of a similar nature, and it is always 1st and 2nd person pronouns which follow an accusative scheme while nouns are on an ergative scheme. The reason is pragmatic. Speech Act participants are most likely to see themselves as initiating or controlling an activity so that their occurrence in A function is morphologically unmarked. Then, an explicit marking, accusative case, is used when they are in O function. The situation is reversed for nouns. By comparison with 1st and 2nd person pronouns they are expected more often to be in O function so that this is left unmarked. Syntactic function A is then distinguished from O by an explicit ergative case suffix. And in each instance, syntactic function S is linked with the unmarked transitive function.

A further possibility is for the head of an NP to be a demonstrative. In languages where there is a split, demonstratives are more likely to pattern with nouns than with 1st and 2nd person pronouns (this is so in Dyirbal).

6c *Bound Pronouns*

The first stages of human language—120,000 years or more ago—would have involved lexemes. Grammatical forms developed out of lexemes, and continue to do so. A set of free forms may develop into a closed grammatical system. For example, free form pronouns may reduce in form and shift in function to become 'bound pronouns', which attach to a word within the VP that fills the predicate slot.

Bound pronouns can be illustrated for Tariana, an Arawak language from north-west Amazonia, which has bound pronominal prefixes to verbs that describe actions (but not to verbs that refer to states). Quoting just singular pronouns for S and A functions, we find:

	free forms as head of NP	bound forms as prefix to verb in VP
1sg	nuha	nu-
2sg	piha	pi-
3sg feminine	duha	du-
3sg non-feminine	diha	di-

Each verb has to make a choice from the system of bound pronominal prefixes. For instance, with verb -*ka*- 'look' and inflection -*ka*, which indicates recent past tense plus visual evidential, we get:

(7) nu-ka-ka I looked
(8) du-ka-ka She looked

The one-word sentence (7) could be a complete utterance. However, (8) only indicates that the subject is feminine. As with sentences involving free form '3rd person 'pronouns'—like (3–4) in English—an NP would have to be included in order to know which 'she' is being referred to. (This is taken up in a few pages time, with sentence (9).)

There is a considerable difference between the two varieties of pronouns. The free forms are separate words, functioning as head of an NP in an argument slot within the clause. They may be modified, and their positioning in the clause may be varied (languages differ with respect to these properties). In contrast, a bound pronoun is (in this language) an affix to either the verb or a modifying auxiliary within the VP, which is in predicate slot within the clause.

Whether or not a language has bound pronouns, any free pronoun has the potential to be omitted if it could be understood from the co-text or context (or maybe by gestures, with just the VP being spoken). A bound pronoun may never be omitted. In Tariana, for instance, each verb describing an action must take a prefix from the system of bound subject prefixes.

Note that when a language has bound pronouns, the corresponding free pronouns will be used rather sparingly, often for emphasis.

It was noted in section 6a that while every language has 1st and 2nd person pronouns, some lack corresponding '3rd person' forms. This only applies for free pronouns; bound pronouns differ. For every VP a choice must be made from the system of bound pronouns and this system must thus cover all eventualities. Besides terms referring to speaker (1st person) and addressee (2nd person) there must be a term for when the subject (or whatever) is neither 1st nor 2nd person.

As a consequence, even if there is no '3rd person' free pronoun, there must be a 'not-1st-or-2nd' term in the system of bound pronouns. This can be illustrated for Warlpiri, from Central Australia, where bound pronouns are suffixes to a modal auxiliary which accompanies the verb within a VP. A selection from the pronoun paradigm is:

	free pronouns	bound pronouns for subject (S or A) function
1sg	ŋaju	-rla
2sg	ñuntu	-npa
3sg	<none>	-∅ (zero)
2du	ñumpala	-npapala
3du	<none>	-pala
2pl	ñurrula	-nkulu
3pl	<none>	-lu

It can be seen that in some languages—such as Tariana—bound pronouns have similar form to free ones, while in other languages—such as Warlpiri—the two kinds of pronoun are rather different from each other.

Every grammatical system has a limited number of terms. One term may have zero realisation—the absence of anything in the slot for that system has a meaning. For example, the number system for count nouns in English has two terms—singular, with zero realisation, and plural, shown by orthographic *-s*. We know that *horse-s* is plural, referring to more than one animal, and we know that, by virtue of its zero suffix, *horse* (really *horse-∅*) is singular, referring to a single animal.

Every term in a system of bound pronouns may have non-zero form, as in Tariana. Or one term may have zero realisation, as in Warlpiri. In this language, if the bound pronoun slot is left empty (rather than being 1sg *-rla*, or 2sg *-npa*, or 3pl *-lu*, etc.) then it must have 3sg reference. Cross-linguistically, if one term in a bound pronoun system has zero realisation, it typically is 3sg.

Note the contrast with free pronouns. There could not be a free pronoun with zero realisation, any more than we could have a zero lexical word, be it noun, verb, or adjective.

Bound forms typically follow the same scheme of argument identification as free forms—accusative if both nouns and pronouns show an accusative pattern, ergative if they both show an ergative one.

Ngiyambaa, a language from New South Wales, has a typical split, with nouns being ergative (one form for S and O, a different one for A) and free 1st and 2nd person pronouns being accusative (one form for S and A, a different one for O). Bound 1st and 2nd person pronouns are accusative, like the corresponding free forms. Ngiyambaa has no free-form 3rd person pronouns. But, of course, the system of bound pronouns must have a '3rd person' term for referring to 'not speaker or addressee'. The interesting feature is that the bound 3rd person forms are ergative, like nouns and unlike 1st and 2nd person pronouns:

	1st and 2nd person free pronouns e.g. 2sg	1st and 2nd person bound pronouns e.g. 2sg	syntactic function	3rd person bound pronouns e.g. 3sg	nouns e.g. 'dog'	
NOM	ŋindu	-ndu	A	-lu	mirri-gu	ERG
			S	-nan	mirri	ABS
ACC	ŋinu:	-nu:	O			

Some languages have bound pronouns just for one syntactic function. An example of this is Latin, illustrated in the paradigm at (5), where verbal inflections code tense, voice, mood, and the person and number of the S or A argument. The most common arrangement is to have two bound pronoun slots within the predicate—either one for S and A and the other for O, or one for S and O and the other for A. Just a few languages have three slots, also including a peripheral argument (an 'indirect object'). The way in which bound pronouns relate to the verbal element varies; in some languages they all precede the verb, in some they all follow it, in others there is a mixture of the two. Occasionally, bound pronouns for A and O functions are fused into a single unit.

Grammatical information can be expressed through affixes or through short grammatical words. For example, syntactic function may be shown by a case system, realised by affixes, or by prepositions, which are separate words. Bound pronouns may be shown as affixes, as in the examples given so far in the section. Or they may be short grammatical words within the VP; this will be illustrated in section 7. Whichever way they are realised, bound pronouns form a closed grammatical system within the predicate in contrast to free pronouns which are head of an NP in a (core or peripheral) argument slot within the clause.

Bound pronouns invariably occur in a fixed order with no scope for variation. Most often the order is determined by syntactic function; for example A before O. In some languages it is determined by person; for example, 1st before 2nd or 3rd, 2nd before 3rd (irrespective of function). Bound pronouns may make the same semantic distinctions as the corresponding free forms, but there are sometimes fewer; for example, free pronouns may have separate dual and plural forms, with bound pronouns merging these. (The opposite happens only occasionally, with bound pronouns showing more distinctions than free ones.)

When discussing Tariana, we noted that the verb *nu-ka-ka* 'I looked' in (7) can be a complete sentence since 1sg bound pronominal prefix *nu-* provides full specification of the S argument. In contrast, *du-ka-ka* 'she looked' in (8) is incomplete; an NP in S function has to be added, in order to know which 'she' is being referred to. For example, (8) can be expanded to:

(9) hema$_S$ du-ka-ka$_{IPr}$
    tapir(feminine) 3sg.feminine.S-look-RECENT.PAST.VISUAL
    The tapir looked

We now have the S argument of this intransitive clause being realised at two places—by the NP *hema* and by *du-* from the system of bound pronominal prefixes. Some linguists have worried over which of these should be considered prior. Arguments can be provided for each alternative:
- The prefix *du-* should be taken as the basic statement of S, since it is a term in an obligatory grammatical system. It is 'cross-referenced' by the NP *hema* 'tapir', which is optional.
- The NP *hema* 'tapir' should be taken as the basic statement of S since it provides the most information. It is 'cross-referenced' by prefix *du-*.

This question concerning priority arises from a stance of analysing surface structure. If, instead, attention is focussed on underlying syntactic structure then the question does not arise. What we have in (9) is:

An intransitive clause consisting of an intransitive predicate (IPr) and an S core argument.
- The IPr relates to a VP which consists of a single verb, with root *ka-* 'look' and suffix *-ka* 'recent past tense plus visual evidential'.
- The S argument is simultaneously expressed by two elements—*hema* 'tapir', which is an NP, and 3sg feminine prefix *du-*, which is attached to the verb. Neither has priority; we simply have double realisation.

6d   The Limited Role of Bound Pronouns

Section 2e outlined three means for marking core arguments, and for knowing which NP is in A function and which is in O function in a transitive clause—(a) the order in which phrasal constituents occur within the clause; (b) marking by adpositions; (c) marking through choice from a case system.

It might now be asked whether the use of bound pronouns should be added as a fourth alternative. The answer to this question is 'no'. Bound pronouns provide only a partial specification when reference is to non-speech-act-participants. As a consequence, they must be augmented by one of (a–c).

Consider a sentence in Murinhpatha from northern Australia:

(10) kardu   lawaŋga   rdam-∅-parl
     man   wallaby   3sgA.PAST-3sgO-strike
     The man struck the wallaby OR The wallaby struck the man

The transitive predicate, *rdam-∅-parl*, has prefixes selected from two systems of bound pronouns—*rdam-* shows 3sgA (fused with past tense) and, in the system for O function, 3sg has zero realisation. This word, *rdam-∅-parl*, could be a full sentence 'he/she struck him/her'. However, this merely states that the protagonists were neither 1st nor 2nd person. When two NPs are added, as in (10), we know who the protagonists were but not who was striking who. Murinhpatha has a choice of two ways for resolving this:
- There is an ergative suffix *-ɹə* which can be added to the NP in A function, if needed for disambiguation.
- NPs can occur in varied order but in order to clarify which NP is in what function in a sentence like (10), the NP in A function will precede the NP in O function.

Some languages have a number of gender distinctions within 3rd person bound pronouns. This can identify arguments if the NPs relating to A and O are of different genders—for example 'boy girl she.A-him.O-thanked'—but not if they belong to the same gender—as in 'duchess girl she.A-her O-thanked'.

In summary, core arguments are marked by any of means (a–c) or by a combination of these. And these means may be augmented—but not replaced—by a system or systems of bound pronouns within the predicate.

In some languages the same bound pronouns which are used for core arguments within a clause may also be added to nouns to show possession within a phrase.

Q In recent years there has arisen the habit of describing languages as 'head marking' or as 'dependent marking'. This distinction is applied to NPs, according to whether there is a mark of possession on the possessor (usually the 'dependent') or on the possessed (usually the 'head').

The same distinction has been applied at clause level, and here it is seriously unhelpful. It involves labelling the predicate as the 'head' of a clause, a practice that was criticised in comment J at the end of section 2. There is then said to be a contrast between languages with bound pronouns within the predicate relating to core arguments ('head marking') and languages lacking bound pronouns but using adpositions or case inflections on NPs to show their syntactic function ('dependent marking').

As has just been shown, bound pronouns play a limited role and have always to be augmented by case or adpositional marking, or by an ordering convention. In the last few decades the overall characterisation of languages as 'head marking' or 'dependent marking' at clause level has gained considerable favour. It is however a false dichotomy, the application of which leads to analyses which lack clarity and insight.

7 Head of a Verb Phrase

The predicate slot in clause structure is normally filled by a verb phrase (VP). Example (4) in section 2b provided illustration of an alternative—found in a minority of clauses in just a few languages—with the intransitive predicate slot (IPr) filled by an NP.

We can now examine the structure of the VP, and in particular what may be in its head slot. Since a clause only has one predicate, but may have two core arguments and several peripheral arguments, the predicate is the focus, within which a great deal of grammatical information is likely to be stated.

Linguists argue whether, for example, tense relates to the whole clause or just to the predicate. If one hears *Sam ran*, does that mean that Sam's running was in the past, or that Sam did running in the past? No matter which alternative is preferred, the grammatical fact is that past tense is—in virtually every language—marked in the VP. (An alternative might be for it to be shown by a special clause-final element.)

7a *Varieties of Structure for a Verb Phrase*

NPs have similar structures across most languages—head noun, adjective modifier(s), possessor modifier, demonstrative or article, relative clause (although there is considerable variation concerning the ordering of elements in an NP). In contrast, each language has its own possibilities for how a VP is made up. It will be useful to examine the different kinds of VP structure in three languages.

A VP will include a verb root (or compound stem or derived stem) plus a number of grammatical elements; these may be affixes or separate words.

In *Tariana* all the grammatical elements in a simple VP are affixes. For a verb referring to an action there must be one prefix, a choice from the system of bound pronominal prefixes relating to the S or A argument (as illustrated in section 6c). Following the verb root there are around 18 suffixal slots; no verb will include choices from all these slots, but most VPs include three or four or five suffixes. For example (where 'm' is masculine gender):

(1) [walikiri]$_S$
     youth(m)
        [di-wasa-nhi-hu-pidana]$_{IPr}$
        3sg.nonfem.S-jump-PRIOR-WITH.BRUSQUE.MOVEMENT-REMOTE.
        PAST.REP
     The youth had reportedly jumped up with a brusque movement

Verbs which refer to states have the same possibilities, except that there is no bound pronominal prefix (and only about a dozen suffixal slots). An example is:

(2) [walikiri]$_S$ [harame-nhi-pu-pidana]$_{IPr}$
     youth(m)   be.scared-PRIOR-REALLY-REMOTE.PAST.REP
     The youth had reportedly been really scared

If the S argument for an intransitive verb of action were 1st or 2nd person, this would be sufficiently shown by the pronominal prefix to the verb, and the VP could be a complete utterance. But for a transitive verb of action, an NP is required to state the O argument. And for an intransitive verb of state, an NP is needed to show the S argument.

In some languages, including Tariana, bound pronouns are affixes to the verb. But any grammatical category may have its terms realised in a variety of ways—as affixes, as separate short grammatical words, or as a mixture of the two. For instance, the index of comparison in English is shown by the suffix -*er* with some adjectives—for example *tall-er*—and by the separate grammatical word *more* with others—for example, *more ordinary*. (A limited number can take either of these; for example, one may say either *stupid-er* or *more stupid*.)

7A VARIETIES OF STRUCTURE FOR A VERB PHRASE

Bound pronouns constitute a closed grammatical system, from which one choice must be made. As mentioned in section 6c, the terms in a system of bound pronouns can be realised as affixes, or short grammatical words, or a mixture of the two. In every instance, they occupy a fixed position within the predicate.

The possibilities may be illustrated for *Jarawara*. This language has two slots in the VP—preceding the head—for bound pronouns. The first—obligatory in a transitive clause—shows the O argument, and the second—obligatory in every clause—shows the S or A argument. These can be illustrated with the transitive verb *mita* 'hear, listen to':

(3) [owa ti-mita]$_{TPr}$
    1sgO 2sgA-hear
    You (sg) hear me

(4) [owa tee mita]$_{TPr}$
    1sgO 2plA hear
    You (pl) hear me

The bound pronouns for S and A arguments in the second VP slot are a mixture. 2sg *ti-*, in (3), and 1sg *o-*, in (5), are prefixes while the plural members of the system, such as 2pl *tee* in (4), are separate words. All the forms in the first VP slot, referring to O function, are separate words—1sg *owa* in (3–4), 3pl *mera* in (6), and so on. In both systems of bound pronouns, 3sg has zero realisation.

The verb in Jarawara can occur with other prefixes, such as *to-* 'away' and *na-* causative, both in (6). It may be used without any suffixes, as in (3–4), or may make a selection from any of about 20 suffixal slots, as illustrated in:

(5) [jimo]$_O$ [∅
    ant(m) 3sgO
    o-nabohe-himari-ka]$_{TPe}$
    1sgA-kill-FAR.PAST.EYEWITNESS.m-DECLARATIVE.m
    I killed an ant long ago

(6) Jima$_O$ [mera ∅
    <tribe(m)> 3plO 3sgA
    to-na-ka-maki-wahe-mata-monaha]$_{TPr}$
    AWAY-CAUS-in.motion-FOLLOWING-THEN-FAR.PAST.
    NONEYEWITNESS.m-REP.m
    He/she is said then to have gone after the Jima people long ago

In the transitive clause (5) the A argument is shown by 1sg prefix *o-*; the lack of an explicit form (a zero term) in the first VP slot indicates that the O argument is 3sg, further specified as *jimo* 'ant' in the pre-predicate NP. In (6) intransitive verb root *-ka-* 'be in motion' is made transitive by causative prefix *na-*. The O argument is shown by NP *Jima*, the name of a tribe, and by 3pl O bound pronoun *mera* in the first prefix slot; note that plural number is shown in the bound pronoun, not in the NP. A zero in the second VP slot indicates that the A argument is 3sg (this refers back to Saba, a man mentioned in the previous sentence of this story).

For each clause in Jarawara the VP must make a choice from the systems of bound pronouns—just from the second slot for an intransitive clause, and from both slots for a transitive clause. Some bound pronouns are prefixes and some are separate grammatical words, but all behave in the same way. They must occur in fixed position, and nothing can come between them.

Fijian has a complex structure for its VP, with the root and more than 15 slots, each realised by short grammatical words. The only obligatory items are bound pronouns. The initial element in every clause is a bound pronoun for S or A function. For example, 1sg *au* in:

(7) [au   rai]$_{\text{IPr}}$
     1sgS   look
     I am looking

Most verbs have two forms—the plain root is used in an intransitive clause, and in a transitive clause the root bears a transitive suffix *-Ci*, where *C* is a consonant determined by the root. Corresponding to intransitive *rai* 'look', we get transitive *rai-ci* 'look at, see'. A transitive verb is followed by a choice from the system of bound pronouns in O function, such as 2sg *i'o* (' indicates a glottal stop) in:

(8) [au   raci-ci   i'o]$_{\text{TPr}}$
     1sgA   look-TRANSITIVE   2sgO
     I am looking at you

3sg bound pronouns are *e* in the S/A paradigm and *'ea* in the O paradigm. However, transitive suffix *-Ci* may fuse with *'ea* giving *-Ca*, as in (9).

An example of a transitive sentence is:

(9) [au   sa   rai-ca   dina   sara   gaa]$_{\text{TPr}}$
     1sgA   ASPECT   look-TRANSITIVE:3sgO   TRULY   VERY   INDEED
          [a   elefadi]$_{\text{O}}$
          ARTICLE   elephant
     I really and truly did see an elephant

Between the subject bound pronoun and the verb there can be a marker of tense or aspect; in (9), *sa* contrasts this moment with a later one. Between a tense/aspect marker and the verb there can be a choice of one (or sometimes more) from a set of pre-head modifiers (such as *via* 'want to, need to' and *rui* 'unusually'). Following the verb within the predicate there are eleven slots for types of modifiers. Three are included in (9)—*dina* 'truly', *sara* 'very, (go) right on, immediately' and *gaa* 'indeed, just'. The A argument is fully specified by 1sg bound pronoun *au*, the first word in the predicate. The O argument is here shown as 3sg by the final *a* of the transitive suffix -*ca*, and by the post-predicate NP *a elefadi*. (Note that each NP commences with an 'article'; this is *a* if the NP head is a noun, and *o* if it is a pronoun or the name of a person or place.)

If a VP consists of a verb root plus an assortment of affixes, such as (1–2) in Tariana, then in many instances the affixes must occur in a fixed order. Fijian has only one suffix (transitive marker -*Ci*), all other items in the predicate being short grammatical words. Nevertheless, the same principle applies—the components of the VP must occur in a fixed order. For example, the VP in (9) consists of a string of six words, and these may not be permuted.

7b   Something Other Than a Verb as Head of a Verb Phrase

In many languages the head of a VP can only be a verb—a transitive verb for a transitive clause and an intransitive verb for an intransitive clause. The only way of using a noun or adjective within a VP is to apply a verbalising derivation to it. In English, for instance, from noun root *hospital* can be derived verb stem *hospital-ise*, and from adjective root *solid* can be derived verb stem *solid-ify*.

A fair number of languages allow further possibilities. Generally, only a verb may be head of a transitive VP, but there are alternatives possible for an intransitive VP. This can be illustrated for the languages exemplified in the last section. *Jarawara*, in fact, permits no further possibilities—the head of a VP must be a verb. But both Tariana and Fijian are more generous, allowing a range of choices for the head of an intransitive predicate.

For *Tariana*, a VP with an intransitive verb of action as head, and a VP with an intransitive verb of state as head were illustrated in (1) and (2) respectively from section 7a. Alternatively, the VP head of an intransitive clause may be a noun, as in an account given in a myth of transmutation:

(10) čiãri$_S$ [kuphe-pidana]$_{IPr}$
       man   fish-REMOTE.PAST.REP
       A man was reportedly a fish

The head of an intransitive VP in Tariana may be any of a variety of words—an intransitive verb, as in (2), or a noun, as in (10), or an adjective, or a demonstrative, or even a free pronoun. A VP whose head is not a verb has the same make-up as a VP whose head is a verb, save that the number of affixal possibilities is more limited; this is simply because of the semantics of the forms involved. Suffixes *-nhi* 'prior', in (1–2), and *-hu* 'with a brusque movement', in (1), would be unlikely following a noun or adjective as VP head, due to incompatibility of meanings. However *-pu* 'really' is quite possible. And so are tense/evidentiality suffixes such as *-pidana* 'remote past reported', in (1–2) and (10). Indeed, it is a choice from this system which enables us to recognise *kuphepidana* in (10) as a VP.

Fijian shows similarities with Tariana. The head of the VP in a transitive clause may only be a verb, with transitive suffix *-Ci*, as in (8–9). But the head of an intransitive VP may be a verb with no suffix, as in (7), or a noun, or an adjective, or a free pronoun. It can extend even further—a full NP (just dropping its article) may be VP head, as in:

(11) [e   sa   [marama   savasavaa]$_{NP}$ sara   gaa]$_{IPr}$ [o
     3sgS   ASPECT   lady   clean   VERY   INDEED   ARTICLE
     Koleta]$_S$
     <person>
     Koleta is indeed a very clean lady

The VP head here consists of an NP with head noun *marama* 'lady' and adjective modifier *savasavaa* 'clean'.

As in Tariana, a VP in Fijian with a non-verb as head may be followed by only a limited selection from the set of intra-VP modifiers available for verbs, for reasons of semantic compatibility. Note that *sara* 'very' and *gaa* 'indeed'—two of the modifiers in (9), where the VP has a verb as head—are included in (11), where there is an NP as VP head.

8   Copula Clauses and Verbless Clauses

As set out in section 2a, all languages have intransitive clauses and transitive clauses. Many—but by no means all—languages have a third clause type:
- *Copula clause*, whose core components are a copula predicate (abbreviated to CPr) and two core arguments—copula subject (CS) and copula complement (CC). For example:

8 COPULA CLAUSES AND VERBLESS CLAUSES

(1) [The owner of the butcher's shop]$_{CS}$ [is]$_{CPr}$ [the secretary of the golf club]$_{CC}$

The important difference between the clause types is that an intransitive or transitive predicate slot is filled by a VP which has reference, whereas a copula predicate slot is filled by a copula verb which has no reference but simply marks a relation between CS and CC.

The CS argument shows similar possibilities to S, A and O arguments for intransitive and transitive clauses—generally an NP, sometimes a complement clause. In contrast, the CC argument has wider possibilities. It is the nature of the CC which indicates the kind of relation between the referent of the CS and the referent of the CC.

The types of relation in English include:

CC	RELATION	EXAMPLE
NP	Identity	[That man in the photo]$_{CS}$ [is]$_{CPr}$ [me/Joseph]$_{CC}$, and (1)
	Description	[My wife]$_{CS}$ [is]$_{CPr}$ [an executive]$_{CC}$
	Naming	[This village]$_{CS}$ [is]$_{CPr}$ [Upper Downing]$_{CC}$
adjective	Attribution	[The manager]$_{CS}$ [is]$_{CPr}$ [wicked]$_{CC}$
possessor	Possession	[The box on the table]$_{CS}$ [is]$_{CPr}$ [Sue's]$_{CC}$
peripheral NP	Benefaction	[The box on the table]$_{CS}$ [is]$_{CPr}$ [for Sue]$_{CC}$
	Location	[The statue]$_{CS}$ [is]$_{CPr}$ [in the village square]$_{CC}$
	Temporal	[Breakfast]$_{CS}$ [is]$_{CPr}$ [at eight o'clock]$_{CC}$

The relation of Identity indicates that CS and CC have the same reference. That of Description states that the referent of the CS is a member of a certain class, described by the CC. In Naming the CC provides the name for the CS.

Besides these possibilities, where the CC slot is filled by an NP (just like S, A, O and CS slots), the CC differs from other arguments in that it can be just an adjective or a possessor (which alternatively function as modifiers to the head of an NP). The relation of Attribution is similar to that of Description—*The manager*$_{CS}$ [*is*]$_{CPr}$ [*wicked*]$_{CC}$ is equivalent to [*The manager*]$_{CS}$ [*is*]$_{CPr}$ [*a wicked person*]$_{CC}$.

It is possible to have a complement clause as CS—for example [*That Arthur is studying hard*]$_{CS}$ [*is*]$_{CPr}$ [*good/a welcome development*]$_{CC}$—or as CC—as in [*The plan*]$_{CS}$ [*is*]$_{CPr}$ [*that Peter should write the foreword*]$_{CC}$.

Languages vary as to which relations are covered by a copula construction. In most instances, the CC may be an NP or an adjective. For it to be an NP plus a preposition, which normally functions as peripheral argument—as in English—is unusual. Many languages require a regular verb here, saying something like 'The statue stands in the village square' or 'Breakfast is served at eight o'clock'.

Whereas intransitive and transitive verbs have reference, a copula verb is something of a dummy, just there to indicate a certain relation between the referents of CS and CC, the nature of the relation being inferred from the nature of these referents. A copula verb is an item upon which to place grammatical information that goes with a referential verb—tense, aspect, evidentiality, modality, bound pronouns, and so on. Quite a few languages may omit the copula verb from a copula clause under certain conditions. For example, in Hungarian the copula is omitted in present tense, when the CS is 3sg, for relations of Identity, Description, and Attribution (but not for Possession or Location).

Some languages lack a copula verb but show some of the relations just illustrated simply by apposition. It is as if the copula predicate slot is permanently left blank (rather then only sometimes left blank, as for Hungarian). Such a 'verbless clause' will have a Verbless Clause Subject (VCS) and Verbless Clause Complement (VCC), parallel to CS and CC. Examples can be provided from Yidiñ, an Australian language:

CC	RELATION	EXAMPLE		
NP	Description	[jugi	yiŋu]$_{VCS}$	[junda]$_{VCC}$
		tree	THIS	stump
		This tree is (just) a stump		
adjective	Attribution	[mayi	yiŋu]$_{VCS}$	[mambu]$_{VCC}$
		fruit	THIS	sour
		This fruit is sour		
possessor	Possession	[guda:ga	ŋuŋu]$_{VCS}$	[waga:l-ni]$_{VCC}$
		dog	THAT	wife-GENITIVE
		That dog is (my) wife's		

To refer to time, for instance, within a verbless clause one could include an appropriate temporal adverb.

Copula and verbless clauses have two core arguments, just like a transitive clause. However, CS/VCS and CC/VCC are very different from A and O. If a language has bound pronouns, then these sometimes include CS but (for all the languages that I have studied) never CC.

8 COPULA CLAUSES AND VERBLESS CLAUSES

It is, of course, necessary to distinguish CS/VCS from CC/VCC and this is most often achieved by ordering (even where this is no strict ordering for A and O). In Jarawara, for instance, A and O NPs can come in either order before the transitive predicate. However, in a copula clause, the CS has to precede the CC, both coming before the predicate. One day I caught a moth and put it outside the door (rather than killing it). A Jarawara friend commented:

(2) [Jobeto]_{CS}   [kiso]_{CC}   [ama-ka]_{CPr}
    <name>   capuchin.monkey   be-DECLARATIVE.m
    Jobeto is (like a) capuchin monkey

The copula verb *ama* in (2) here indicates not description but rather similarity. My action reminded the speaker of a capuchin monkey, which catches moths (and eats them).

The one exception to this ordering principle in Jarawara is that, for the Naming relation, the CS must precede the copula predicate and the CC must follow it. A Jarawara man visited a neighbouring tribe, the Suruwaha, and later reported that:

(3) [mee   kaa   awa   ino]_{CS} [ama-ka]_{CPr}   [maone]_{CC}
    2pl   POSSESSOR   tapir name   be-DECLARATIVE.m   <name>
    Their name for tapir is 'maone'

A CS argument generally has similar syntactic properties to an S argument. A rare exception is found in Ainu, originally spoken in northern Japan, where the bound pronominal prefix for CS is the same as that for A, different from that for S.

A number of languages have more than one copula verb. Most commonly, one will just refer to a state and the other to coming into a state, similar to *be* and *become* in English. For example:

(4) [My son]_{CS} [is]_{CPr} [a doctor]_{CC}
(5) [My son]_{CS} [became]_{CPr} [a doctor]_{CC} (by passing his exams)

Some languages have different copulas for different types of relation. And there may be a negative copula, with a quite different form from the positive one.

8a *Contrasting Copula Complement with Non-verbal VP Head*

There are two techniques, grammatically quite different, for describing some state:

(i) By a copula clause such as, in English, [*The weather*]$_{CS}$ [*is*]$_{CPr}$ [*unusually bad*]$_{CC}$.

(ii) By using an NP (which may be just a noun), or an adjective, as head of the VP in an intransitive clause. An example from Fijian is:

(6) [e   rui   caa]$_{IPr}$ [a   dra'i]$_S$
    3sgS   UNUSUALLY   bad   ARTICLE   weather
    The weather is unusually bad (lit. the weather unusually is-bad-ing)

The fact that adjective *caa* 'bad' is preceded by 3sg bound pronoun *e* and pre-predicate-head modifier *rui* 'unusually' shows that it is here functioning as head of an intransitive VP.

In the majority of instances, each language employs just one of these techniques.

– In *Jarawara* the head of a VP must be a verb; as a consequence, (ii) does not occur. This language has a well-developed copula clause construction—with two copula verbs, *ama* 'be' (and 'be like'), illustrated in (2–3), and *-ha-* 'become'—and employs technique (i).

– In *Fijian*, the head of a VP can be any of a variety of non-verbal elements, with technique (ii)—illustrated in (11) from section 7 and (6) above—being much used. There is no copula clause construction, for technique (i).

However, there are languages which employ both techniques, and these include *Tariana*. The intransitive clause (7)—repeated from (10) in section 7—with a noun as head of the VP, illustrates technique (ii):

(7) čiãri$_S$ [kuphe-pidana]$_{IPr}$
    man   fish-REMOTE.PAST.REP
    A man was reportedly a fish

And technique (i) is shown by the copula clause construction:

(8) čiãri$_{CS}$ kuphe$_{CC}$ [di-dia-pidana]$_{CPr}$
    man   fish   3sg.nonfem.CS-become-REMOTE.PAST.REP
    A man reportedly became a fish

Both sentences refer to the kind of transmutation which can occur in a myth. Using *kuphe* 'fish' as head of an intransitive predicate in (7) indicates a state. In contrast, using *kuphe* as CC for copula verb *-dia-* 'become' in (8) describes the actual change that occurred. Note that since the verb in (8) describes an action, it takes a bound pronominal prefix for the CS argument. A tense/evidentiality suffix, here *-pidana* 'remote past reported', occurs on all types of predicates—transitive, intransitive, and copula.

R   A predicate whose head is a nominal element could be termed a 'nominal predicate'; this would apply to (11) from section 7 and (6–7) from this one.

Unfortunately, the term 'nominal predicate' is often used in a quite different way, for copula-verb-plus-copula-complement within a copula construction. For instance, in $Sapir_{CS}$ was_{CPr} [*a great linguist*]$_{CC}$, the sequence *was a great linguist* could be termed a 'nominal predicate'.

This is a relic of following the practice of philosophers in regarding a sentence as consisting of 'subject' and 'everything else', this being labelled 'predicate'. (See comment C towards the end of section 2a.) Most linguists have abandoned such an analysis, and should now refrain from the pervasive mislabelling of a CC (plus its copula verb) a 'nominal predicate'.

The difference between (7) and (8) in Tariana (other languages show a similar contrast) underlines the importance of employing precise and unambiguous terminology.

9 Types of Intransitive Subject, S

Intransitive subject (S) is identified as the sole core argument in an intransitive clause, irrespective of its reference or role. A transitive clause has two core arguments and here pragmatic properties serve to distinguish them. Transitive subject (A) is the core argument whose referent has the potential to initiate or control the activity or state. The other core argument is then in transitive object (O) function (its referent may or may not be physically or mentally affected by the activity).

No language has different marking for S, A, O across all types of NP. (Some languages have such 'tripartite' marking for just some types of words; for example, proper names of people.) In the great majority of languages we either get S marked like A (nominative), differently from O (accusative), or else S marked like O (absolutive), differently from A (ergative).

However, there are exceptions—some languages have 'split-S' marking and a few have 'fluid-S' marking. These will now be explained.

9a   Split-S Marking

For some intransitive verbs, the referent of the S argument could initiate or control the activity or state, just as the referent of an A argument may for a transitive verb. For other intransitive verbs it is unlikely to be able to do so.

As a reflection of this, there are languages where—instead of always marking S in the same way as A (a nominative/accusative system), or always marking S in the same way as O (an absolutive/ergative system)—some intransitive verbs mark S, their sole core argument, like A while other intransitive verbs mark it like O. These two subdivisions of S can be called Sa and So respectively.

A clear example comes from Warekena, an Arawak language of northern Brazil, which has two sets of bound pronouns. A transitive verb bears a prefix showing the A argument, and a suffix showing the O argument, as in:

(1)   nu-yutsia-pi
       1sgA-hit-2sgO
       I hit you (sg)

Intransitive verbs divide into two sets. For the Sa set, the S argument is shown by a bound pronominal prefix, identical to the A argument for a transitive verb; for example:

(2)   nu-tapa
       1sgSa-walk
       I walk

For the So set, the S argument is shown by a bound pronominal suffix, identical to the O argument for a transitive verb; for example:

(3)   yeletua-pi
       be.tired-2sgSo
       You (sg) are tired

What are the implications of this? Can we infer that the choice of marking for an S argument goes beyond syntax, and is entirely a question of meaning? Close examination—cross-linguistically—of the content of Sa and So verb sets shows that this is not the case.

There is certainly a correlation between meaning and set membership. In Warekena, intransitive verbs of motion and rest are Sa, since this is something which the referent of the S argument is likely to control—'walk', 'run', 'return', 'sit, live, stay', and many more. Other Sa verbs include 'blow nose', 'stretch', and 'speak'. Intransitive verbs describing states (from which modifying adjectives may be derived) are So; this is something for which the referent of the S argument is unlikely to be in control—'be tired', 'be soft', 'be good, beautiful', 'be shy', and so on. Other So verbs include 'be hurt', 'be breathless', and 'survive, remain alive'.

However, there are a fair number of incongruities. The Sa set includes verbs such as 'die', 'sneeze', 'snore', and 'become humid', where one would not imagine control to be involved. And the So includes verbs such as 'be married', 'play music', 'be silent', and 'appear', where control is rather likely.

Other split-S languages behave in a similar way. In Hidatsa, a Siouan language, most verbs in the Sa class do involve control, but there are also 'die', 'forget', and 'have hiccups'. Most of those in the So set do not involve control, but there are also 'stand', 'roll over', and 'dress up' which surely do.

It has been stressed that S, A, O, CS, CC (and VCS, VCC) belong to syntax, not to semantics. 'A' does not stand for 'agent'. Rather, A (an abbreviation for transitive subject) is a syntactic argument; it corresponds to a fair number of roles at the semantic level—Agent, Donor, Speaker, Perceiver, and so on.

In the same way, Sa and So are syntactic arguments. Each intransitive verb belongs to either the Sa set or the So set; there is no choice involved (depending, say, on the sense of a verb in a particular instance of use). A split of S marking is certainly semantically motivated, but it is not semantically determined.

(It is reasonable to enquire whether, for a 'split-S language', it is necessary to recognise an S argument. Could we not make do just with A and O arguments—a transitive clause must include both of these and an intransitive clause either of them. In fact, this is not feasible. In every split-S language, Sa and So do group together as an S category, which has different grammatical properties from A and from O.)

9b Fluid-S Marking

Some activities described by intransitive verbs are generally controlled, while others are seldom or never controlled. And there are quite a few activities which can be either purposeful or involuntary. One may cough on purpose (to clear one's throat, or perhaps just to indicate disagreement) or be subject to a fit of coughing; one may bump into someone deliberately or by accident.

A number of languages divide intransitive verbs into three sets:
- Sa—S always marked like A for a transitive verb.
- So—S always marked like O for a transitive verb.
- Can be marked in either way.

The third set includes verbs referring to actions where there may or may not be control; whether or not there is control in a particular instance of use determines the choice of Sa or So marking. Consider a verb which may be glossed either as 'slip' or 'slide'. What we get is:
- So marking for meaning 'slip', as when someone unfortunately slips over and hurts themself.
- Sa making for meaning 'slide', as when someone joyously slides on skates across the ice.

One of the best-documented fluid-S systems in found in the North-east Caucasian language Batsbi (or Tsova-Tush). For NPs whose heads are nouns, 3rd person pronouns or demonstratives, ergative case is used for A while absolutive case is used for O and all S. However, when 1st and 2nd person pronouns are involved as S, we find:

(i) Sa verbs, which are only acceptable with a pronominal S in ergative form. These include 'jump', 'crawl', 'rest', 'swear', 'talk nonsense', 'complain', and 'think'.

(ii) So verbs, which are only acceptable with a pronominal S in absolutive form. These include 'tremble', 'be hungry', 'be cold', 'fit in (through a small space)', and 'melt'.

(iii) Verbs which may have a pronominal S with either marking, depending on whether the situation described by this particular use of the verb is achieved deliberately or happens involuntarily.

Set (iii) can be illustrated with the verb *vuiž/vož* 'fall'. The 1sg pronoun has ergative form *as* when in A function, and absolutive form *so* when in O function. The appropriate form of the pronoun is suffixed to an intransitive verb. It may also be included, optionally, as a free pronoun preceding the predicate.

(4) (as) vuiž-n-as
(1sg.ERGATIVE) fall-AORIST-1sg.ERGATIVE
I fell down, on purpose

(5) (so) vož-en-so
(1sg.ABSOLUTIVE) fall-AORIST-1sg.ABSOLUTIVE
I fell down, by accident

Other intransitive verbs with variable marking (depending on whether an action is deliberate or unintentional) include 'get drunk', 'touch', 'be late', and 'behave'. Also the following, where the variable marking is characterised by different senses of the verbs:

VERB	SENSE WITH ERG PRONOUN	SENSE WITH ABS PRONOUN
gagar	take care of oneself	get taken care of
keba(d)dalar	boast	be praised
kot:dalar	run around anxiously, doing things	be troubled, worried

It can be seen that, while superficially similar, split-S and fluid-S marking are in fact fundamentally different. Split-S is a syntactic division, each intransitive verb taking just Sa marking or just So marking; as stated before, the split is semantically motivated but not semantically predictable.

In contrast, fluid-S marking is a semantic matter. The two possibilities—marking S like A in a transitive clause, or marking S like O—are available for each intransitive verb. Which is chosen depends on the circumstances for that instance of use; put roughly, whether or not there is control. For some intransitive verbs there is always control; for others this is never likely. For a middle set, control is an option, whether or not this is exercised being shown by choice of marking.

S Various names have been attached to what I call split-S and fluid-S marking; these include 'active/inactive' and 'active/stative'. (Also 'agentive/patientive', which further extends the muddled practice of using semantic labels 'agent' and 'patient' for syntactic arguments A and O; see comment H at the end of section 2d, and also comment K at the end of section 3.) A difficulty is that, typically, a single label groups together split-S marking—which is a syntactic phenomenon—and fluid-S making—which is a semantic phenomenon. To avoid terminological confusion, it seems safest to employ self-explanatory labels 'split-S' and 'fluid-S'.

T Labels 'unergative' and 'unaccusative' were introduced in the late 1970s and have been applied to a range of quite different contrasts:

		'UNERGATIVE' USED FOR	'UNACCUSATIVE' USED FOR
I	In languages with ambitransitive verbs—section 2c	Ambitransitive verbs of type S = A.	Ambitransitive verbs of type S = O.
II	In languages with split-S marking	Intransitive verbs taking Sa marking.	Intransitive verbs taking So marking.
III	Generally	Verbs typically taking an antipassive derivation—A becomes S, and O becomes an optional peripheral argument.	Verbs typically taking a passive derivation—O becomes S, and A becomes an optional peripheral argument.
IV	Generally	Verbs typically taking an applicative derivation—S becomes A, and an erstwhile peripheral argument becomes O.	Verbs typically taking a causative derivation—S becomes O, and a new, causer, argument is introduced as A.

It will be seen that S and A are linked in the 'unergative' column, as are S and O in the 'unaccusative' one. Nevertheless the type of syntactic correlation are quite different for each of I–IV, and using the same terminology for them is undesirable.

The use of 'unergative' and 'unaccusative' has now waned, but they are still present in the literature. To avoid confusion, these terms should be avoided, or else carefully explained in each instance of use. In fact, they are not needed.

10 The Sentence and Above

A sentence has a grammatical structure. And there will be a semantic relation between its constituent clauses. These are discussed in turn. We then pay attention to discourse (and paragraph).

10a *The Syntax of Clause Linking*

Each sentence includes a Main clause. This is an intransitive, transitive, or copula clause—with predicate and an appropriate set of arguments—without any marker of coordination or dependency. Indeed, a simple sentence consists just of a Main clause.

Section 5 discussed the two kinds of subordinate clauses—complement clause that fills an argument slot, and relative clause that modifies the head of an NP which is in an argument slot.

We can now deal with subordinate clauses which are linked to the Main clause. Some of the possibilities can be illustrated from English, with main clauses in blue.

(1) After the volcano erupted, the town lost electricity
(2) The town lost electricity, after the volcano erupted

The Adjoined clause, *after the volcano erupted*, has the structure of a main clause, plus a marker of subordination, *after*. In (1) the order of clauses mirrors the order of events; nevertheless (2) is equally acceptable, the event sequence being clearly indicated by *after*.

The clauses making up a sentence often share an argument with the same reference. Rather than this being stated several times, in full, some occurrences may be replaced by a third person pronoun:

(3) After he had won the lottery, John gave up his job
(4) After John had won the lottery, he gave up his job

In (3) John is stated in the Main clause and replaced by a cataphoric (forwards looking) pronoun *he* in the preceding Adjoined clause. An alternative is possible here; in (4), John is stated in the Adjoined clause and replaced by an anaphoric (backwards looking) pronoun *he* in the Main clause.

However, when the Main clause comes first, only the anaphoric option is available:

(5)   John gave up his job, after he had won the lottery

That is, we cannot have, with the same meaning:

   *He gave up his job, after John had won the lottery

He here could only be anaphoric, referring to someone (not John) identified in an earlier sentence of the discourse.

If, in English, Main and Adjoined clauses share the same (S or A) subject, the Adjoined clause need not have the structure of a main clause, its subordinate status being shown by an initial subordinate marker plus *-ing* on the first word of the VP. Temporal sequence is illustrated in (6) and reason in (7).

(6)   After having won the lottery, John gave up his job
(7)   As a result of having won the lottery, John gave up his job

The subordinate marker can be omitted from either of these, giving:

(8)   Having won the lottery, John gave up his job

This is ambiguous between a temporal and a reason sense.

An Adjoined clause may be marked just by *-ing* even if it doesn't have the same subject as the Main clause. Sentence (9) indicates reason, while (10) combines reason with temporal sequence.

(9)   The weather being inclement, we thought it best to cancel the picnic
(10) The company having gone into bankruptcy, Roy found himself out of work

U   Comment P in section 5b described how 'infinitive', a term from Latin grammar, was inappropriately taken over into English grammar by early scholars who approached English as if it were a variant of Latin. This term is much used in contemporary work on European languages but is generally shunned as inappropriate by modern linguists producing sophisticated grammars of languages from other parts of the world.

The related term 'finite' is of more recent origin but is likewise unnecessary and potentially confusing. It appears to have been coined in the 1790s by Lindley Murray in a grammar intended for schools, and was apparently intended to be the complement of 'infinitive'; the term 'finitive' would have been more appropriate. Essentially, 'finite clause' is simply a more high-flown name for 'Main clause' (and 'finite verb' for 'Main verb'). Many different definitions have been provided: 'any clause which is not an infinitive or a participle'; or 'expressing or implying tense, number, person, and mood'; or just 'having tense' (in which case THAT complement clauses would have to be considered as 'finite'). In the late nineteenth century, 'finite' was joined by 'non-finite'.

The ways in which terms 'finite' and 'non-finite' are used are varied and confusing. And they are unnecessary. Label 'Main clause' is clear and sufficient, and is to be preferred.

10b   *The Semantics of Clause Linking*

An indispensable requirement of linguistic analysis is to clearly distinguish between syntax and semantics. For instance, syntactic arguments must not be confused with semantic roles, as happens when transitive subject function (conveniently abbreviated to 'A') is called 'Agent'. As explained in section 3, Agent (for verbs of AFFECT) is just one of the semantic roles linked to the syntactic argument slot A. Other roles associated with slot A include Experiencer, Perceiver, and Cogitator, which could scarcely be described as agents.

Syntactic analysis and semantic interpretation are not always congruent. For instance, in the sentence [*The handyman*]$_{NP:A}$ [*has begun*]$_{VP:TPr}$ [*to paint the fence*]$_{CoCl:O}$, the main verb is *begin*, and *paint* is the verb in the TO complement clause which fills the O slot in the main clause. But, looking at the meaning of the sentence, what the handyman is engaged in is *painting*, with *begin* providing semantic qualification of this, indicating what phase this activity is at.

A similar situation is found at the level of sentence structure. In sentences such as (1–5) there are two clauses, each with the structure of a Main clause. One bears a marker of subordination—here *after*—and is Adjoined to the

other, which is the Main clause of the sentence (in blue in each example). This is at the level of syntax. However, when we look at the meaning of a bi-clausal sentence, it is useful to recognise:
– The Focal clause, which specifies the central activity.
– The Supporting clause, which supplies some temporal or logical or other qualification.

Either clause may have attached to it a Marker showing the type of semantic relation which holds between the two clauses—Mf is a marker attached to the Focal clause, and Ms is a marker attached to the Supporting clause. Syntactically, the clause without a marker is the Main clause and the clause with the marker is the Adjoined clause. This can be illustrated for the relation of Contrast:

	Ms	SUPPORTING CLAUSE = ADJOINED CLAUSE	Mf	FOCAL CLAUSE = MAIN CLAUSE
(11)	Although	Adam is corpulent	—	he is very fit
(12)	Although	he is corpulent	—	Adam is very fit

	Ms	SUPPORTING CLAUSE = MAIN CLAUSE	Mf	FOCAL CLAUSE = ADJOINED CLAUSE
(13)	—	Adam is corpulent	but	he is very fit

The order of clauses could be reversed in (12). Similar to (3–5), anaphoric *he* is acceptable in all sentences, and cataphoric *he* when the Main clause comes last as in (12), but not where the main clauses comes first, in (13). That is, we could not have, with the same meaning, **He is corpulent but Adam is very fit*.

We can now illustrate the relation of Consequence:

	Ms	SUPPORTING CLAUSE = ADJOINED CLAUSE	Mf	FOCAL CLAUSE = MAIN CLAUSE
(14)	Because	Eve knows Greek	—	she can read the Gospels in the original
(15)	Because	She knows Greek	—	Eve can read the Gospels in the original

	Ms	SUPPORTING CLAUSE = MAIN CLAUSE	Mf	FOCAL CLAUSE = ADJOINED CLAUSE
(16)	—	Eve knows Greek	(and) thus	she can read the Gospels in the original

Similar comments apply.

Some inter-clausal semantic relations are shown in English by a marker just on the supporting clause; for example, *after* and *before* for Relative Time; *lest* for Possible Consequence; *if* and *unless* for Conditional.

It is likely that all languages have some means for marking relations of Time, Consequence, and Addition. They may be indicated by separate grammatical words, as in English, or by affixes (sometimes, special senses of cases). Addition may be just by apposition of clauses. Not every language has an explicit marking for Contrast, this relation then being shown by contrastive intonation (a quite different intonation from that used for addition by apposition).

10C *Above the Sentence*

Grammar—with its structures and principles and (as is often said) rules—stops at the sentence. But, when someone speaks, it is not in a staccato sequence of isolated sentences. They are talking *about* something, which we can call the 'Topic'. A sequence of sentences will each say something concerning the topic, and the sentences are integrated together in order to produce a smooth and coherent discourse.

The following is a speaker telling part of the story of Alice:

(17)

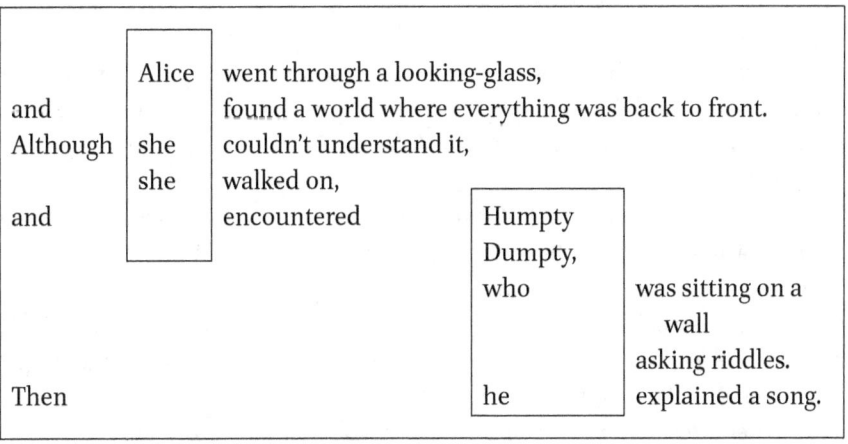

For the beginning part of the discourse the Topic is *Alice*. This name is stated in the first line and referred to by anaphoric pronoun *she* in the third and fourth lines. As mentioned in section 2f, English operates with an S/A pivot—if two clauses share an argument which is in S or A function in each, its second occurrence may be omitted, as in the second and fifth lines. A new Topic,

Humpty Dumpty, is introduced in the fifth line (overlapping with *Alice* here) and is then referred to by *who* and *he*, with the A argument omitted from the penultimate line.

A topic is most often nominal, but it may be verbal, as when someone is describing the sports activities of a group of people:

(18)

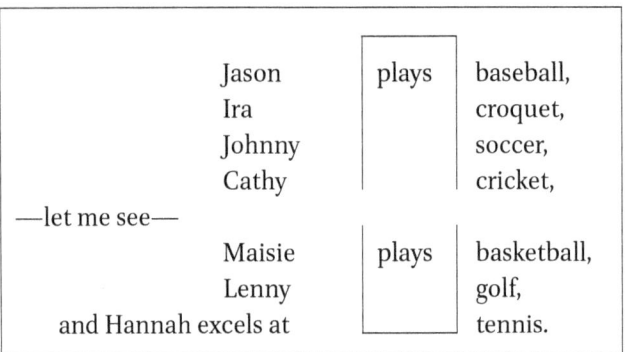

Verb *plays* links together the lines of this discourse, the continuity being temporarily interrupted only by the thought-gathering interpolation *let me see*. The verb does not need to be stated in lines 2, 3, 4, and 7; in the final line *playing* is understood.

A discourse may have just one speaker or several (each supplying one or more 'utterances'). For example, in (17)—or in (18)—two or more speakers could alternate in telling the story, each maintaining the continuity begun by the previous speaker.

Language is essentially a spoken medium. People have been writing it down for only a fraction of its history and—even in the most literate societies—writing is secondary to speaking. We can clearly discern the organisation of spoken discourse, but the way in which it is written—with full stops, colons, semi-colons, commas, and division into paragraphs—is to a great extent subjective, essentially an artefact, a matter of style.

A writer attempting to make their prose readily understandable will opt for short sentences. But a pedant would join several together (for example, this sentence and the previous one). If one topic links a hundred clauses covering several pages, a pedant may write it as one paragraph consisting of long sentences. A more user-friendly author will break things up, so that the reader receives them in manageable chunks. The message would be the same but its delivery different. (This is akin to the use of intonation in speech. A steady, boring drawl. Or an engaging and varying tone of voice, highlighting the important points and contrasts.) (A pedant would make the previous parenthesis into a single sentence, with a semi-colon or colon after 'speech' and a comma after 'drawl'.)

• • •

The basis of language is words and grammar. Speakers work with a range of structural patterns, and techniques for inserting lexical words into them. In this way they can expound an unlimited array of thoughts, observations, feelings, instructions, wishes, hopes, and so on. Meanings are communicated through the medium of sounds for a spoken language, or manual and facial configurations for a signed language.

This book, and other typological studies, outline the basics of a language. By itself this is simply bare. Every spoken (or signed) utterance adds embellishments indicating attitude, commitment, degree of certainty or doubt, involvement, and other interpersonal stances. Canonical phonological expressions may be adjusted to reflect the situation—a trembly voice where fear is involved, a warm soothing tone for endearment, clipped speech to indicate the peremptory nature of a command, a deeper tone to convey satisfaction.

The voice can be modulated in many ways. But there is much more than this involved in an act of communication—how the head is held, gaze of the eyes, twist of the mouth. And the way the speaker's whole body is comported. This will tie in with the intonation used—stiff and upright for a stern command, leaning towards the addressee for a bashful request, relaxed for a casual comment.

Language is a holistic experience, building upon the infrastructure outlined in this and similar works.

Commentary and Notes

Many of the topics discussed above are dealt with in fair detail in the following books which I have published:
- BLT—*Basic linguistic theory*, Vols. 1–3. 2010–12. Oxford: Oxford University Press.
- *Ergativity*. 1994. Cambridge: Cambridge University Press.
- ANATEG—*A new approach to English grammar, on semantic principles*. 1st edition, 1991; and ASATEG—*A semantic approach to English grammar*. 2nd edition, 2005. Oxford: Oxford University Press.

Many topics are also dealt with, in similar vein, by:
- AoG—*The art of grammar: A practical guide*, by Alexandra Y. Aikhenvald. 2015. Oxford: Oxford University Press.
- *The Cambridge Handbook of Linguistic Typology*, edited by Alexandra Y. Aikhenvald, and R. M. W. Dixon. 2017. Cambridge: Cambridge University Press.

Information on Dyirbal is based on my grammar *The Dyirbal Language of North Queensland* (Cambridge: Cambridge University Press 1972) and my knowledge of the language.

As noted in the Preface, *Essence* is conceived of as a consolidation document, suitable for those who have thoroughly studied BLT, or AoG, or similar works by other authors.

Preliminary Note

Important methodological principles which were clearly enunciated in BLT, particularly in Chapter 1 of Volume 1, are not repeated here. These include:
- A grammar is an integrated system, and all analytic decisions must be based on language-internal criteria (not solely on semantics). For instance, the word classes for a particular language are recognised on internal grammatical criteria within that language, with meaning playing a secondary role. (See BLT volume 1, pages 24–27.)
- The world includes a multiplicity of contrasts and distinctions but a grammar is necessarily of limited size. As a consequence, one grammatical category may code a number of disparate semantic contrasts. The way to pursue linguistic analysis is *not* to list everything which has a certain grammatical property but rather to uncover the underlying semantic contrasts for a given language and investigate how these are mapped onto the grammar. For example, if one lists the verbs in English which take a particular variety of complement clause, there appears to be nothing in common to them, no principle involved. The key is to approach this from the other end. That is, to examine the various semantic types of verbs and the meaning relations their subsets express, and then the ways these correlate semantically with the meanings of complement clause types. (See BLT volume 1, pages 27–35.)

Essence aims to integrate grammatical features, predominantly of a syntactic nature. Many topics, which were fully dealt with in BLT and/or AoG, only receive tangential mention here; they include (among quite a few others):

demonstratives, possession, tense, and aspect, negation, comparative constructions, and questions. Also scarcely mentioned in *Essence* are the mechanics of valency-changing derivations (see particularly Table 22.2 on page 173 of BLT volume 3). There are just a few instances where *Essence* goes into more detail (with fuller exemplification) than BLT; for example, section 9b on Fluid-S marking.

Notes to Sections

2b Examples from Mandarin Chinese and Nootka are repeated, with correction, from BLT 1: 111; original sources are given on BLT 1: 179.
2e Japanese examples from Kuno (1973: 3, 6). Malayalam examples from Asher and Kumari (1997: 193). For 'marked nominative' see *Ergativity* 63–7 and König 2008. Note that some languages have none of (a–c) but one just infers which transitive argument is in A function and which is in O function from the context of usage—BLT 2: 119.
2f For a survey of the recurrent links between S and O, and also those between S and A, see Aikhenvald and Dixon 2011: 143–69, and *Ergativity* 111–142.
3 There is a detailed account of Semantic Types and their Semantic Roles, in English, throughout ANATEG and ASATEG.
4a Japanese examples from Kuno (1973: 5); Malayalam from Asher and Kumari (1997: 63, 193–6).
4c Information on Tongan repeated from BLT 1: 99–100, 179.
5c For explanation of the inclusion of *it* before a THAT complement clause for verbs of LIKING, as in example (27), see ASATEG 160–3, ANATEG 155–9.
5d For types of complement clauses in different languages see BLT 2: 393. Jarawara example from Dixon (2004: 447). For complementation strategies see BLT 2: 405–13.
6b Further intricacies within splits in case marking can be explained in terms of the 'nominal hierarchy' which goes as follows: 1st person pronouns > 2nd person pronouns > 3rd person pronouns and demonstratives > proper names > common nouns (with human > other animate > inanimate). The further to the left an item is, the more likely it is to follow an accusative scheme, and the further to the right the more likely it is to follow an ergative scheme. Justification for the hierarchy, and more detail on attested splits, is in *Ergativity* 83–94 and BLT 2: 137–42.
6c Tariana from Aikhenvald (2003: 122, and p.c.). Warlpiri from Hale (1974: 5). Ngiyambaa from Donaldson (1980: 120–6).

Some languages can have four bound pronominal positions within the verb; but this is extremely rare; an example from Abaza is quoted in BLT 2: 214.

6d Murinhpatha from Walsh (1976: 406); see also Walsh (2012), Nordlinger (2011), and *Ergativity* 58–9. This language has a complex predicate structure. Street (1987) recognises 35 verbal conjugations. In example (10), verb *-parl* 'strike' belongs to conjugation 19 which takes *rdam-* as 3sg subject fused with past tense. Interestingly, the object bound pronoun intervenes between the auxiliary element, here *rdam-*, and the lexical root *-parl*.

Working in the 1980s, Walsh (2012) noted that ergative suffix *-ɹə* was quite common. In her fieldwork from thirty years later, Nordlinger (2011: 717–9) found it used only rarely. This is plainly a matter of language change.

7,8 Tariana from Aikhenvald (2003 and p.c.) and BLT 2: 163. Jarawara from Dixon (2004 and personal knowledge). Fijian from Dixon (1988 and personal knowledge).

8 This section is based on BLT 2, chapter 14. Yidiñ from Dixon (1977 and personal knowledge). For Ainu see BLT 2: 166–7.

A copula construction must have two arguments, CS and CC. In some languages there is a variant with just CS; it means 'CS exists'. However, if there is a verb 'exist' which is always restricted to one argument, then this is an intransitive verb, not a copula.

Note that if a language has several copula verbs, only one of them may be omitted in particular circumstances.

8a Fijian does have occasional clauses consisting just of two NPs; generally, one of them includes an interrogative or demonstrative, as in '[Where]$_{NP}$ (sc. is) [your residence]$_{NP}$' or '[That]$_{NP}$ (sc. is) [the method for planting plantains]$_{NP}$'. See Dixon (1988: 241–2).

9a Information on Warekena from Aikhenvald (1998 and p.c.). For more on split-S and fluid-S systems (with information on sources) see *Ergativity* 71–82. Also see Mithun (1991).

Exemplification of how Sa and So group together as an S argument is in *Ergativity* 75.

9b Information on Batsbi (Tsova-Tush) from Holisky (1987). She investigated 233 intransitive verbs and found that 78 were only accepted with an ergative pronoun (the Sa set), 31 only with an absolutive pronoun (the So set), and 124 with either. Of the latter, ergative was preferred for 36, absolutive was preferred for 27, and the two kinds of pronouns were deemed equally acceptable for 61.

The tabulation in box T at the end of section 9 is from Dixon (1999: 327).
10a For 'infinite' and 'finite' see BLT 1: 80. The definition of finite as 'expressing or implying tense, number, person, and mood' is from Zandvoort (1966: 35); that as 'having tense' from Chalker and Weiner 1994: 151.

References

Aikhenvald, Alexandra Y. 1998. 'Warekena', pp. 225–440 of *Handbook of Amazonian languages*, Vol. 4, edited by Desmond C. Derbyshire and Geoffrey K. Pullum. Berlin: Mouton de Gruyter.

Aikhenvald, Alexandra Y. 2003. *A grammar of Tariana from northwest Amazonia*. Cambridge: Cambridge University Press.

Aikhenvald, Alexandra Y. 2015. *The Art of Grammar: A Practical Guide*. Oxford: Oxford University Press.

Aikhenvald, Alexandra Y., and Dixon, R. M. W. 2011. *Language at large: Essay on syntax and semantics*. Leiden: Brill.

Aikhenvald, Alexandra Y., and Dixon, R. M. W. 2017. Editors of *The Cambridge Handbook of Linguistic Typology*, Cambridge: Cambridge University Press.

Asher, R. E., and Kumari, T. C. 1997. *Malayalam*. London: Routledge.

Bloomfield, Leonard. 1933. *Language*. New York: Holt.

Chalker, Sylvia, and Weiner, Edmund. 1994. *The Oxford dictionary of English grammar*. Oxford: Oxford University Press.

Dixon, R. M. W. 1972. *The Dyirbal language of North Queensland*. Cambridge: Cambridge University Press.

Dixon, R. M. W. 1977. *A grammar of Yidiñ*. Cambridge: Cambridge University Press.

Dixon, R. M. W. 1988. *A grammar of Boumaa Fijian*. Chicago: University of Chicago Press.

Dixon, R. M. W. 1991. *A New Approach to English Grammar, on Semantic Principles*. Oxford: Oxford University Press.

Dixon, R. M. W. 1994, *Ergativity*. Cambridge: Cambridge University Press.

Dixon, R. M. W. 1999. 'Semantic roles and syntactic functions: The semantic basis for a typology', *CLS* 35,2: 323–41.

Dixon, R. M. W. 2004. *The Jarawara language of southern Amazonia*. Oxford: Oxford University Press.

Dixon, R. M. W. 2005. *A Semantic Approach to English Grammar*. Oxford: Oxford University Press.

Dixon, R. M. W. 2010–2012, *Basic Linguistic Theory*, vols. 1–3. Oxford: Oxford University Press.

Donaldson, Tamsin. 1980. *Ngiyambaa: the language of the Wangaaybuwan*. Cambridge: Cambridge University Press.

Hale, K. L. 1974. *Warlpiri grammar*. Alice Springs: Institute for Aboriginal Development. [17 pp.]

Holisky, Dee Ann. 1987. 'The case of the intransitive subject in Tsova-Tush (Batsbi)', *Lingua* 71: 103–32.

König, Christa. 2008. *Case in Africa*. Oxford: Oxford University Press.

Kuno, Susumu. 1973. *The structure of the Japanese language*. Cambridge, MA: The MIT Press.

Mithun, Marianne. 1991. 'Active/agentive case marking and its motivation', *Language* 67: 510–46.

Nordlinger, Rachel. 2011. 'Transitivity in Murrinh-patha', *Studies in Language* 35: 702–34.

Sapir, Edward. 1921. *Language*. New York: Harcourt Brace.

Shopen, Timothy. 1985. Editor of *Language typology and syntactic description*, 3 volumes. Cambridge: Cambridge University Press.

Shopen, Timothy. 2007. Editor of *Language typology and syntactic description*, 3 volumes, 2nd edition. Cambridge: Cambridge University Press.

Street, Chester S. 1987. *An introduction to the language and culture of the Murrinh-patha*. Darwin: Summer Institute of Linguistics, Australian Aborigines Branch.

Walsh, Michael. 1976. 'Ergative, locative and instrumental case inflections: Murinypata', pp. 405–8 of *Grammatical categories in Australian languages*, edited by R. M. W. Dixon. Canberra: Australian Institute of Aboriginal Studies, and New Jersey: Humanities Press.

Walsh, Michel James. 2012. *The Muɹinyapata language of north-west Australia*. Munich: Lincom Europa. [Mis-titled publication of 1976 PhD thesis *The Muɹinypata language of north-west Australia*.]

Zandvoort, R. W. 1966. *A handbook of English grammar*. London: Longmans.

Index

A, transitive subject function 3–8, 20–24, 32–34, 65–6
absolutive case 9–13, 26, 32–34, 47–49, 65–66, 68, 80
Accompaniment peripheral argument 31
accusative case 9–14, 27–29, 48–49, 51, 65–66, 79
active/inactive marking 69
active/stative marking 69
Addressee semantic role 19, 22, 24–25, 34
adjoined clause 71–74
adpositions 2, 9, 25–28, 53–55; *see also* prepositions, postpositions
AFFECT semantic type 19, 20, 24–25, 34, 41, 73
Agent semantic role 8, 19–21, 24, 67, 73
agentive/patientive marking 69
Aikhenvald, Alexandra Y. VII, 78–81
Ainu 63, 80
ambitransitive verbs of type S = A 6–7, 14, 70
ambitransitive verbs of type S = O 6–7, 14, 70
anaphoric elements 45–48, 71–72, 74–75
ANNOYING semantic type 23, 43
Art of grammar, The (AoG) VII–VIII, 78, 81
Asher, R. E. 79, 81
ATTENTION semantic type 19, 21, 24, 33–34, 41–42, 44
attribution relation 61–62
Avar 34

Basic Linguistic Theory (BLT) VII–VIII, 77–80
Batsbi (Tsova-Tush) 68, 80, 82
benefaction relation 61
Benefactive peripheral argument 25, 31
Bloomfield, Leonard VII, 81
BLT (*Basic Linguistic Theory*) VII–VIII, 77–80
bound pronouns 46, 49–59, 62–66, 80

CA (common argument in a relative clause construction) 36–37
case marking 10–14, 25–29, 48–49, 52–53, 55, 75, 79

cataphora 71, 74
CC (copula complement function) 60–65, 67, 80
Chalker, Sylvia 81
clause 3–7; 17–18, 35; *see also* adjoined clause, complement clause, focal clause, main clause, relative clause, subordinate clause, supporting clause
Cogitator semantic role 19–22, 24, 34, 41, 73
comitative 26, 29, 47
common argument in a relative clause construction (CA) 36–37
complement clause (CoCl) 35, 37–45, 61, 71, 73, 78–79
constituent order 3–4, 9, 11, 28–29, 33, 54–55, 63
copula clause 60–65, 71, 80
copula complement function (CC) 60–65, 67, 80
copula subject function (CS) 60–65, 67, 80
core arguments 3–12, 17–18, 26, 32–35, 37, 41, 53–54, 60–62, 65–66
core of clause 3–12, 17–18, 25
Course semantic role 19, 21, 24, 41–42
CS (copula subject function) 60–65, 67, 80

dative 26–27, 32–34
DECIDING semantic type 19, 21, 24, 41
Decision-maker semantic role 19–21, 24
'dependent marking' 55
derivation 4, 14–18, 32, 59, 70, 79
description relation 61–63
discourse 71–76
Donaldson, Tamsin 79, 82
Donor semantic role 19–20, 24, 44, 67
Dyirbal 6, 10–11, 13, 26, 28, 46–49, 78, 81

E (extension to core function) 32–34
ergative case 9–14, 26, 32–34, 48–49, 51, 54, 68, 80
Experiencer semantic role 19, 22–24, 33–34, 42–43, 73
extended intransitive clause 32–34
extended transitive clause 32–34
extension to core (E) 32–34

Fijian   58–60, 64, 80
finite   73, 81
fluid-S marking   9, 67–69, 79–80
focal clause   74
(FOR) TO complement clause   38–45, 40, 73
free pronouns   45–55, 60

Gift semantic role   19–21, 24, 34
GIVING semantic type   19–20, 24, 41

Hale, K. L.   79, 82
'head marking'   55
head of a noun phrase   4–5, 14
head of a verb phrase   4–5, 14, 55–60
head, confused ideas about   55
Hidatsa   67
Holisky, Dee Ann   80, 82
Hungarian   62

identity relation   61–62
Impression semantic role   19, 21, 24, 33, 41–42
infinitive   40, 73
ING complement clause   38–45
inner peripheral argument   30–31
Instrumental peripheral argument   25–26, 31
intransitive clause   3, 6–8, 59, 64–65, 67
intransitive predicate   3–7, 17, 55, 59–61
intransitive subject function (S)   3–8, 32–33, 65–70; see also fluid-S marking, split-S marking

Japanese   7, 25–26, 79, 82
Jarawara   44, 57–59, 63–64, 80–81

König, Christa   79, 82
Kumari, T. C.   79, 81
Kuno, Susumu   79, 82

Latin   6, 11–12, 16–17, 27–29, 40, 46, 52, 73
LIKING semantic type   19, 22–23, 32–34, 42–44, 79
location relation   61–62
locative   26–27

main clause   1, 3, 36–38, 71–74
Malayalam   10, 27–29, 79, 81

marker of clause linking   71–75
Means peripheral argument   31
Medium semantic role   19, 22, 24
Message semantic role   19, 22, 24, 41–42
Mithun, Marianne   80, 82
MOTION semantic type   37, 41
Murinh-patha   54, 80, 82

naming relation   61, 63
Ngiyambaa   51, 79, 82
nominal predicate   65
nominative case   9–14, 27, 29, 48, 65–66, 79
Nordlinger, Rachel   80, 82
noun phrase (NP)   4–5, 14, 25–34

O (transitive object function)   3–8, 20–24, 32–34, 65–66
outer peripheral argument   31

Perceiver semantic role   19–21, 24, 31, 34, 41, 67, 73
peripheral argument   3, 10, 20, 25–34, 41, 52, 61–62, 70
phrase   4–5, 14–15, 17–18, 28–29
possession relation   61–62
postpositions   9, 26–27
predicate   3–8, 17, 54–55, 59–61
prepositions   9, 20, 22, 26–33, 52, 61–62
pronouns   45–55
Purpose peripheral argument   31, 34

Recipient semantic role   19–21, 24, 34
relative clause (RC)   35–37
REST semantic type   30, 41
root   15–18, 59

S (intransitive subject)   3–8, 32–33, 65–70; see also fluid-S marking, split-S marking
Sapir, Edward   VII, 82
semantic roles   18–25, 30, 33–34, 41–43, 73, 79
semantic types   18–25, 30, 33–34, 41–44, 78–79
sentence   3–4, 6, 71–77
Shopen, Timothy   VII, 82
Source peripheral argument   31
Speaker semantic role   19, 22, 24, 41–42, 67

SPEAKING semantic type   19–20, 22, 24, 34, 41–42, 67, 77
split-S marking   9, 65–7, 69, 70, 80
stem   15–16, 56, 59
Stimulus semantic role   19, 22–24, 33, 42–43
storeys   17–18, 35
Street, Chester S.   80, 82
subordinate clause   71–75
supporting clause   74–75

Target semantic role   19–20, 24–25, 34
Tariana   49–51, 53, 56, 59–60, 64–65, 78, 80–81
temporal relation   61–62
THAT complement clause   35, 38–45, 73, 79
THINKING semantic type   19, 21, 34, 41, 44
Thought semantic role   19, 21, 24, 34, 41
Tongan   32–34, 79
topic of discourse   75–78
Topic peripheral argument   31
transitive clause   3, 6–9, 20, 33, 59
transitive object function (O)   3–8, 20–24, 32–34, 65–66
transitive predicate   3–8, 17, 19, 54

transitive subject function (A)   3–8, 20–24, 32–34, 65–66
Tsova-Tush (Batsbi)   68, 80, 82

unaccusative   70
unergative   70

verb phrase (VP)   4–5, 14, 55–60
verbless clause complement function (VCC)   62–63, 67
verbless clause subject function (VCS)   62–63, 67
verbless clause   62

Walsh, Michael   80, 82
Warekena   66, 80–81
Warlpiri   50–51, 79, 82
Weiner, Edmund   81
word formation   15–18
word order   11

Yidiñ   62, 80

Zandvoort, R. W.   81–82

Books by R. M. W. Dixon

Books on Linguistics

Linguistic Science and Logic
What *is* Language? A New Approach to Linguistic Description
The Dyirbal Language of North Queensland
A Grammar of Yidiñ
The Languages of Australia
Where Have All the Adjectives Gone? And Other Essays in Semantics and Syntax
Searching for Aboriginal Languages: Memoirs of a Field Worker
A Grammar of Boumaa Fijian
A New Approach to English Grammar, on Semantic Principles
Words of Our Country: Stories, Place Names and Vocabulary in Yidiny
Ergativity
The Rise and Fall of Languages
Australian Languages: Their Nature and Development
The Jarawara Language of Southern Amazonia
A Semantic Approach to English Grammar
Basic Linguistic Theory, Vol. 1, Methodology
Basic Linguistic Theory, Vol. 2, Grammatical Topics
Basic Linguistic Theory, Vol. 3, Further Grammatical Topics
I am a Linguist
Making New Words: Morphological Derivation in English
Edible Gender, Mother-in-law Style and Other Grammatical Wonders: Studies in Dyirbal, Yidiñ and Warrgamay
Are Some Languages Better than Others?
"We Used to Eat People": Revelations of a Fiji Islands Traditional Village
The Unmasking of English Dictionaries
Australia's Original Languages: An Introduction
English Prepositions: Their Meanings and Uses

with Alexandra Y. Aikhenvald
Language at Large: Essays on Syntax and Semantics

with Grace Koch
Dyirbal Song Poetry: The Oral Literature of an Australian Rainforest People

with Bruce Moore, W. S. Ramson and Mandy Thomas
Australian Aboriginal Words in English: Their Origin and Meaning

Books on Music
with John Godrich
Recording the Blues

with John Godrich and Howard Rye
Blues and Gospel Records, 1890–1943

Novels (under the Name Hosanna Brown)
I Spy, You Die
Death upon a Spear

Editor of Books on Linguistics
Grammatical Categories in Australian Languages
Studies in Ergativity

with Barry J. Blake
Handbook of Australian Languages, Vols 1–5

with Martin Duwell
The Honey Ant Men's Love Song, and Other Aboriginal Song Poems
Little Eva at Moonlight Creek: Further Aboriginal Song Poems

with Alexandra Y. Aikhenvald
The Amazonian Languages
Changing Valency: Case studies in Transitivity
Areal Diffusion and Genetic Inheritance: Problems in Comparative Linguistics
Word: A Cross-linguistic Typology
Studies in Evidentiality
Adjective Classes: A Cross-linguistic Typology
Serial Verb Constructions: A Cross-linguistic Typology
Complementation: A Cross-linguistic Typology
Grammars in Contact: A Cross-linguistic Typology
The Semantics of Clause-linking: A Cross-linguistic Typology
Possession and Ownership: A Cross-linguistic Typology
The Grammar of Knowledge: A Cross-linguistic Typology
The Cambridge Handbook of Linguistic Typology
Commands: A Cross-linguistic Typology

with Alexandra Y. Aikhenvald and Nerida Jarkey
The Integration of Language and Society: A Cross-linguistic Typology

with Alexandra Y. Aikhenvald and Masayuki Onishi
Non-canonical Marking of Subjects and Objects

with Alexandra Y. Aikhenvald and Nathan White
Phonological Word and Grammatical Word: A Cross-linguistic Typology

www.ingramcontent.com/pod-product-compliance
Lightning Source LLC
Chambersburg PA
CBHW071410290426
44108CB00014B/1759